The Beatles

John Tobler

The Beatles

John Tobler

Photographic Acknowledgments
Cyrus Andrews, London 7, 8 left, 8 right, 9, 38, 39, 40 bottom, 41 top, 41 bottom, 43, 45, 47, 48 bottom, 51, 59, 62 bottom, 123; Associated Newspapers, London 52, 56 bottom, 65 top, 70, 80 top, 82 bottom, 93, 95 top, 97, 99, 104 top, 104 bottom, 106, 115 top, 168, 178, 181 bottom, 182 top; Camera Press, London 67 top, 95 bottom, 119, 126, 141 top, 141 bottom, 163, 167 bottom, 173 top; Frank Driggs Collection, New York 10, 11 bottom, 12, 13 bottom, 16, 17 top, 23 top; EMI Records, London 32, 103, 167 top; EMI Records-John Kelly, London 84, 85, 86, 87; Flair Photography, Bushey Heath 6; Bill Harry, London 17 bottom, 27 bottom; Richard Mathews, Liverpool 18, 24 top, 24 bottom, 25 top, 25 bottom, 26, 27 top, 28 top, 30, 31; National Film Archive, London 54, 60 top, 68 bottom, 78, 89 bottom, 92, 94, 110, 111 bottom, 116, 117, 121 top, 124, 125, 130, 134, 135 top, 148, 171 top, 171 bottom; The Photo Source/Central Press 60 bottom, 88; The Photo Source/ C.L.I. 118 bottom; The Photo Source/Fox Fotos 48 top, 50, 55 top, 56 top, 57, 77, 96 top, 98, 166; The Photo Source/ Keystone 13 top, 14, 20, 21, 29, 49, 53 bottom, 58 bottom, 62 top, 63, 65 bottom, 66, 67 bottom, 72, 73 top, 73 bottom, 75 top, 75 bottom, 76 top, 76 bottom, 80 bottom, 81, 82 top, 96 bottom, 100 top, 100 bottom, 101, 107, 113 bottom, 114, 118 top, 122, 159 top, 160, 161, 170, 174, 175, 177; Photofeatures/ Relay, London 44, 46, 61, 69, 71, 83, 89 top, 90, 91, 105, 108, 112, 127 bottom, 128 top, 131, 133 top, 136 bottom, 137, 150, 151, 154–5, 157 top, 158, 162 top, 162 bottom, 169; Barry Plummer, Ascot 127 top, 128 bottom, 129, 133 bottom, 139 top, 142, 143, 149, 152; Popperfoto, London 11 top, 15, 33, 37; A. Proudlove, Liverpool 14–15; Rex Features, London back cover, title page, 19, 34 top, 34 bottom, 35, 36, 42 bottom, 53 top, 79, 132, 138, 144 bottom, 145 top, 145 bottom, 152–3, 155 top, 156, 164, 165, 179, 180, 181 top; David J. Smith Collection, Royston 22, 23 bottom, 28 bottom; Syndication International, London front cover.

**This edition produced exclusively for
W H Smith**

Published by
Deans International Publishing
52–54 Southwark Street, London SE1 1UA
A division of The Hamlyn Publishing Group Limited
London · New York · Sydney · Toronto

Copyright © The Hamlyn Publishing Group Limited 1984
ISBN 0 603 03573 6

Printed in Italy

Contents

Introduction

Before 1964 the city of Liverpool, in the northwest of England, was a dot on the map as far as most of the world was concerned – a sizeable place, but with no exceptional features, and certainly not the first city that came to mind when England was mentioned.

Now, some twenty years later, the city of Liverpool is regarded as one of the most famous places in the British Isles, and this elevation to a place of international importance (at least among a certain section of the community) occurred in 1964, when a quartet of Liverpudlian youths, having successfully overcome all opposition locally in the previous year, found themselves the successors to Elvis Presley (whom they had idolized) as the foremost

Left to right: Ringo, Paul, George (front) and John.

act in popular music. Within a few months, they would even overtake the achievements of Presley, and during the 1960s (a quite remarkable decade, whose memory will surely remain when succeeding periods have been forgotten), the name of The Beatles brought England, and specifically Liverpool, to a prominence in popular music it had never enjoyed before. After the Beatle era, America regained much of the ground it had lost (in rock music terms), but twenty years later, it has still failed to completely eradicate the impression made by The Beatles, who spearheaded the 'Merseybeat' (Liverpool stands on the River Mersey) invasion of America and in their wake allowed dozens of other British musicians to achieve international stardom.

With rock'n'roll music (a totally American conception) only around ten years old, almost all British rock'n'roll could be seen, even at the time, as watered-down imitations of the real thing. One of the exceptions to this was Cliff Richard, the British Presley equivalent, who had managed to make at least one significant record, *Move It*, and in the continued absence of Elvis in person, had amassed a fairly substantial fan following of rock'n'roll addicts who desperately wanted personal contact with an idol of their own.

Presley had not been the first American to make an impression in Britain – that distinction belonged to Bill Haley, whose *Rock Around The Clock* had inspired an outbreak of high spirits (or evil spirits, according to the older generations) among a British youth that had been subjected to rationing and similar deprivations after the Second World War. Haley's music was heavily rhythmic, a mixture of white country & Western and black blues, with a predominant ability to make listeners tap their feet and dance, although not in the traditional manner of waltzes, fox trots and quicksteps, but with rather less physical contact and infinitely less inhibition. Before he arrived in Britain, Haley was regarded almost as a deity, but once he was seen as an obviously middle-aged man with a faintly ridiculous kiss curl, his popularity rapidly waned with his British fans.

Haley fell sharply from grace, and while Presley was still idolized *in absentia*, his

The famous collarless jacket modelled here by John Lennon.

spell in the U.S. Army reduced his following in Britain to a smaller, if still substantial, body. After rock'n'roll had made its mark (despite doubters suggesting it was no more than a five-minute wonder), it began to broaden in scope and appeal, and by 1960, had become perceptibly less offensive to adults. This was especially true of the United States, where all but a few of the original rock'n'roll heroes were swiftly consigned to the scrap heap and replaced by a new generation of idols in many cases aimed squarely by the controlling older generation at a youth who had used rock'n'roll as a weapon in their rebellion against the establishment.

In Britain, where there was little home-grown rock'n'roll worthy of the name before The Beatle era, record buyers largely conformed to the American pattern, but on the other hand, a significant nucleus who had enjoyed the early rock'n'roll years, and found the generally watery substitutes they were offered unsatisfying, began exploring to discover other types of music with which they could identify. In general terms, this largely meant music made by black people, whose ethnic musical roots had been partially plundered to produce rock'n'roll in the first place, and although the acquisition of American records was by no means either simple or cheap in 1960, those who

felt they needed it were able, sometimes painstakingly, to buy and hear black music.

Although it was probably far less obvious at the time, Liverpool possessed a major advantage over most other British cities, because a large number of ships from America would make it their first port of call after crossing the Atlantic, and the sailors would often bring American records with them, which would find their way, either as gifts or in exchange for money, into local hands. The essentially international population led to there being music from all parts of the world available on Merseyside at least as early as it reached London, with the result that living there gave greater and earlier access to new trends than living in, for example, Birmingham, which had double Liverpool's population, but a much less tran-

Right: A beaming Ringo Starr.

Far right: George Harrison.

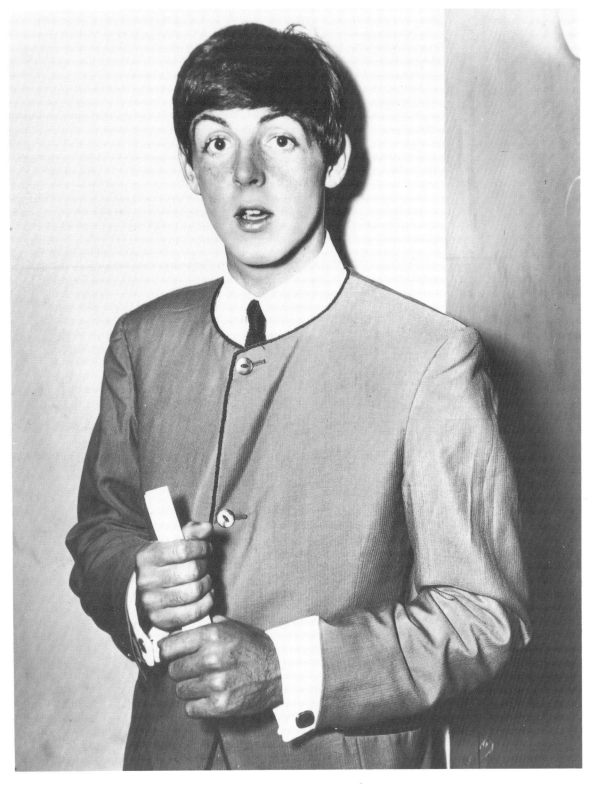

Left: Innocence personified – Paul McCartney as a young Beatle.

sient and international mixture of races at the time, since mobility was still limited in the aftermath of the Second World War.

In this unique city (unique in European terms – it was no coincidence that after the boom in popular music centred around Liverpool, the American equivalent came from another port, San Francisco, with an equally cosmopolitan population), four young white boys grew up from differing backgrounds to become The Beatles. They could not possibly have known that they would make as significant an impression on twentieth century culture as giants in other cultural spheres like Picasso, Marilyn Monroe or Sir Laurence Olivier, but because their particular talents were so accessible to so many, The Beatles have become symptomatic of their era in a way that no other popular musicians have succeeded in doing, and when all their predecessors, contemporaries and successors have been forgotten, their name will be remembered. This is their story.

The Early Years (1940-1960)

Although he was the last to join the group, Ringo Starr was the oldest of the Beatles. He was born on July 7, 1940, during an air raid in a part of Liverpool known as The Dingle. His parents, Richard Starkey and Elsie Gleave, split up and divorced three years after his birth. As a result, the young Ritchie (he was named Richard after his father) spent a lot of his childhood with his paternal grandparents, and rarely saw his father thereafter.

When he was six years old young Richard Starkey was rushed to hospital with a burst appendix, which led immediately to peritonitis. After an emergency operation, the child lay in a coma for some weeks, and altogether spent a year in hospital. When Ritchie was twelve, his mother married Harry Graves, a Liverpool Corporation painter. By that time, the boy was attending Dingle Vale Secondary School, but his earlier health problems kept him from shining scholastically. At the age of thirteen Ritchie caught pleurisy and spent two years in hospital, after which he never returned to school. With an incomplete education and apparently prone to severe illness, the boy was hardly the most promising of employees. Nevertheless, Ritchie Starkey was by all accounts a remarkably cheerful teenager and, although it took some time, he eventually found work as a messenger with British Railways (as it was then known), but after a few weeks he decided to leave. This was followed by a spell working as a barman on ferry boats before his stepfather got him a job with a local engineering firm, Hunts, where he became an apprentice fitter. This was where music entered his life for the first time, when, with a fellow apprentice, he began what was known as the Eddie Clayton Skiffle Group, immediately gravitating towards the drums. Although the group was formed to entertain the other employees of Hunts during their dinner hour, Ritchie and Eddie and their colleagues were well aware that Lonnie Donegan's single *Rock Island Line*, had reached the American Top Ten during the first half of 1956, and had achieved a similar position in Britain. By the end of 1956 Donegan had three Top Ten singles, plus an EP and an album in the charts. There was quite obviously money to be made from skiffle if one were sufficiently good at playing it, and Ritchie Starkey took it seriously enough to want a real drum kit instead of the array of non-musical objects he was forced to use at the start.

Right: A youthful Richard Starkey.

His first kit, which cost £10, was bought for him by his stepfather but this was soon ousted by a brand new kit, which cost the princely sum (for that time) of £100. By 1959 Ritchie had been invited to join a notable local band led by Rory Storm. Storm was regarded by his peers as one of the finest performers from Liverpool in the early 1960s. It was during his time with Storm and his group, the Hurricanes, that Ritchie Starkey became Ringo Starr – Ringo because of the large number of rings he wore on his fingers, and Starr because it sounded appropriate to a show business personality, and also in order that his drum solo at Butlin's Holiday Camp could be billed as 'Starr Time'. It was when the Hurricanes were booked for a season at Butlin's that Ringo had to make the momentous decision to leave his regular job at Hunts.

Subsequently, Storm's group made the trip to Hamburg to become resident at the Kaiserkeller, one of several dives on the infamous and vice-ridden Reeperbahn, which was where Ringo first became

Left: Ringo holding a bottle and a somewhat less cheerful friend during the mid-1950s.

11

Above: Harry and Elsie Graves, Ringo's mother and stepfather, pictured in 1959.

her sister Mimi – herself married but childless, and who adored her young nephew – got Julia to let John live with her and her husband George, which he did from before he reached school age. It seems that John was probably fortunate to have such a doting, but disciplined, aunt as Mimi. Her husband was also extremely fond of the boy. With his uncle's help, John Lennon could read and write only a few months after starting school at Dovedale Primary, near Penny Lane, when he was four.

Like any small boy, Lennon was in a 'gang' at school, his particular henchmen being Pete Shotton and Ivan Vaughan, who also attended Dovedale Primary, and with whom he would indulge in such pursuits as stealing sweets from shops and accepting 'dares' that would probably have terrified their parents/guardians had they been aware of them. It was also discovered during his primary school years that John Lennon had poor eyesight, which inevitably affected his sporting activities. When he was twelve years old, Lennon began to attend Quarry Bank Grammar School, with Pete Shotton, and their names were synonymous with disorder and attempted disruptions of the school curriculum. This seems to have been the result of John's mother starting to become a significant influence on his life. Although he still lived with his aunt, John enjoyed going to stay for weekends with his mother, who encouraged his rebelliousness and apparently contradicted some of the instructions Mimi gave him. Unfortunately, this all resulted in John failing his 'O' Level exams but with some help from the school's headmaster, he was accepted at the local Art College.

By this time, Lennon and Pete Shotton, like most other boys of their age, had become aware of rock'n'roll and particularly skiffle, and had also taken to wearing 'teddy boy' clothes – long draped jackets with velvet collars, plus tight 'drainpipe' trousers, and thick crepe-soled shoes. John began to be interested in learning to play the guitar, and this led to the formation of a skiffle group known as the Quarrymen (after the name of John's school), whose early members included Pete Shotton and Ivan Vaughan. The group began playing together at the start of 1956, with a repertoire of songs usually

friendly with The Beatles. By the summer of 1962, he was back on Merseyside with the Hurricanes. Not long afterwards, he was invited to join The Beatles. . . .

John Lennon was born a few months after Ringo, also during an air raid, on October 9, 1940. His father, Fred, worked as a steward on ocean-going ships, and the day after his wedding to Julia Stanley, Fred spent three months away on a ship to the West Indies. When John was born, no one knew where Fred was, and even when he did return, it was briefly. Before long, the money his employers had been sending to Julia dried up. Later, when Julia met another man whom she wanted to marry, associated with Lonnie Donegan, although their performances were few and far between and generally took place at youth clubs and church garden fêtes. One such occasion was where John Lennon was introduced for the first time to Paul McCartney by their mutual friend Ivan Vaughan. The year was 1957.

Paul McCartney's actual first name is James, after his father, but he was known as Paul to avoid family confusion. He was born on June 18, 1942 – the only Beatle to be born in hospital. This was due not to his being from a moneyed family, but rather because his mother, Mary, had been one of the hospital's nursing sisters before she married Paul's father. Two years later the McCartneys produced another son, Michael (later professionally known as Mike McGear when he was a member of the poetry/rock trio, Scaffold). Paul was apparently a model pupil at his infant school, and passed the eleven plus exam without difficulty, which enabled him to attend the Liverpool Institute, the oldest local grammar school, where he seemingly excelled in academic subjects and was very popular. However, in 1955 Mary McCartney was suddenly stricken with cancer and died, leaving a gaping void in the McCartney family.

As his father had in earlier days led a small jazz group, the Jim Mac Band, Paul was used to hearing music, but it was when he saw Lonnie Donegan appearing at the Liverpool Empire in 1956 that he became keenly interested and craved a guitar of his own. Paul had also taken to wearing 'teddy boy' clothes in homage to his musical idols, and could impersonate Little Richard vocally with some accuracy by the time he was fifteen years old. However, in comparison with John Lennon, Paul McCartney's formative years, apart from his mother's tragic death, were fairly straightforward.

When he went with Ivan Vaughan to the Woolton Parish Church fête in 1957, Paul watched the Quarrymen going through their simplistic repertoire and went to meet them afterwards. He could already play several complete tunes on guitar and knew the words to rock'n'roll hits of the day like *Twenty Flight Rock* and *Be Bop-A-Lula*. He also knew several guitar chords, which impressed comparative beginners like the Quarrymen.

Paul seemed to be in a higher class musically, despite the fact that he was two years younger than most of the Quarrymen. He could even tune his own guitar – a very significant accomplishment for the era – and as a result, he was not immediately invited to join the Quarrymen, since it was felt that as he was too advanced. Eventually, of course, the offer was made, and Paul accepted it.

The group was booked to play at a local jazz venue that had opened earlier in Mathew Street, near Liverpool's city centre. There, a former cellar warehouse, used during the Second World War as an air raid shelter and later simply as store for various goods, had been turned into a jazz

Top: The Quarrymen, with John at the microphone, and Pete Shotton (with blond hair).

Above: Mrs. Mary McCartney with her two children – Paul (left) and Michael.

Above and opposite: The school photograph of the lower school of the Liverpool Institute, April 1956, with several notables included. On this page, reading from left, are Michael McCartney (ringed front row), Paul McCartney (ringed back row), long-time Beatle associate Neil Aspinall (ringed third row down), Quarrymen member Len Garry (ringed, third on Neil Aspinall's left).

Opposite page, reading from right, are George Harrison (ringed back row), TV newsreader Peter Sissons (ringed back row), and John Lennon's boyhood friend (and sometime Quarryman) Ivan Vaughan (ringed back row).

Right: George Harrison in the mid-50s with his first guitar.

club and the cellar's subterranean location made the choice of 'The Cavern' as the name of the Mathew Street club a natural and obvious one. Jazz was the main item on the musical menu, while rock'n'roll was frowned upon due to its supposed musical impurity, although skiffle, which was seen to be closely derived from jazz, was tolerated. This affected the Quarrymen during their first gig at the Cavern – after they had played songs associated with Elvis Presley the group were handed a note by the management instructing them not to play any more rock'n'roll.

The gig took place at the end of 1957 – within a year, skiffle would have been largely forgotten.

A little while later, in early 1958, a school friend of Paul McCartney's named George Harrison joined the Quarrymen. George was born on February 25, 1943, at the home of his parents, Harold and Louise (née French) Harrison, the youngest of the couple's four children. Although neither was aware of it until some time later, George and John Lennon were pupils at Dovedale Primary School at the same time, although John was obviously some years ahead of George. Next, George found himself at the Liverpool Institute, a year behind Paul McCartney, but with a similar taste in teddy boy clothing. He was also extremely impressed by Lonnie Donegan's music, and convinced his mother to buy him a very cheap guitar, which, with continual practice, he soon outgrew, and asked for a better one costing £30 which his mother also managed to provide. George organized a group composed of one of his brothers and several friends, and the Rebels (as they were known) even played a gig at a local British Legion club.

As George and Paul McCartney took the same bus to the Institute, they soon became friendly, especially after discovering their mutual interest in the guitar. Paul encouraged his young friend to come to see the Quarrymen, and George, who had practiced playing the instrumental hits of the day at great length until he was impressively proficient, was happy to associate with a real group. When he showed John Lennon how well he could play *Raunchy*, a current single which was in the American Top Ten in three differ-

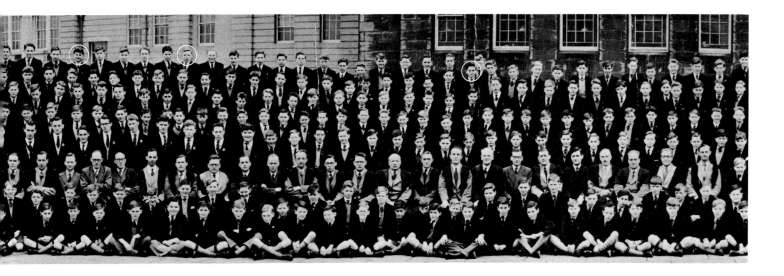

Left: Mrs. Mimi Smith, aunt of John Lennon, and later keeper of his M.B.E. at her Liverpool home.

ent versions simultaneously, John was impressed. His ability to discover new guitar chords was also useful to John and Paul who had both independently begun to write primitive, but original songs, and when George joined the Quarrymen on a more or less permanent basis, three of those who would become The Beatles were together.

Of course, they were all still attending either school or college at the time. John Lennon was finding Art College only marginally more interesting than school, and was to some extent rebelling against

Mimi, and playing off his mother, Julia, against her until Julia was run over and killed by a car during July 1958. Although obviously deeply affected by his mother's death, John apparently refused to show his emotions, retreating into heavy drinking and developing an even more caustic and cruel sense of humour than he had previously shown. However, by the end of 1958, John had acquired a steady girlfriend, a fellow Art College student named Cynthia Powell, who was from a much more well-to-do family than any of John's friends. Their early relationship

Above: A gig by the Quarrymen in Liverpool, 1956. Paul McCartney (left) and John Lennon at the microphones.

largely consisted of John being sarcastic at her expense but by the end of 1958 they began going steady and it seemed almost as if Cynthia was seen by John as a replacement for his dead mother, as he was extremely possessive of her.

Their relationship developed through 1959 during which time the main interest of John, Paul and George remained the Quarrymen – although since the reason for the name had vanished when John left Quarrybank School, the group played under several different names around this period. They continued to play at parties and working men's clubs, usually for little or no financial reward. When they entered a talent contest, calling themselves Johnny and the Moondogs, they were chosen as the act to represent Liverpool in the final held in Manchester. Despite reaching the final, nothing of any note resulted for the group, and not long after-wards, their drummer left. This was also when the first-known recording by the group was made – of the Buddy Holly hit, *That'll Be The Day* – and nearly a quarter of a century later, Paul McCartney bought it for a reported £5000 after he had taken out an injunction to prevent the record being sold at auction to the highest bidder. The one obviously missing in-gredient was a drummer, although the purist reader might wonder how a group could manage without a bass player. Both positions would soon be filled.

John's best male friend at Art College was Stuart Sutcliffe, who was born in Scotland in 1940. Stu, as he was known, wasn't simply a teddy boy, but preferred to develop an individual look, which was fuelled by his consuming passion for art and literature. He was also exceptionally talented as a painter. Sutcliffe also felt it important that he should join the group in which his best friend, John Lennon, played. One major problem stood in the way of Stu simply joining John, Paul and George – he had neither a bass nor a set of drums, and he also lacked the wherewithal to buy an instrument. Sutcliffe would never have opted to be a drummer, as drummers are largely invisible on stage, but he was eventually able to acquire a bass guitar when one of his paintings was selected to be hung in an exhibition at the well-known local Walker Art Gallery, and at the end of the exhibition, was bought for the princely sum of £65.

Later Stu and John briefly shared a flat, and remained very good friends – while Paul and George were still at the Institute, John and Stu would spend much of their time at a coffee bar known as the Jaca-randa, which was owned and run by Allan Williams, who appears to have been an entrepreneur in numerous fields, without achieving huge success in any of them. Williams agreed to help Johnny and the Moondogs to improve their image and hopefully their fortunes by acting in a

Left: The Silver Beatles auditioning for Larry Parnes. From left: Stu Sutcliffe, John Lennon, Paul McCartney, stand-in-drummer Johnny Hutch, and George Harrison.

neo-managerial capacity, in return for which he might ask the boys to perform tasks for him. The first priority was to find a drummer, who arrived in the shape of a fork-lift truck driver in his mid-thirties named Thomas Moore. Despite his unlikely background, Tommy, as he was known, was quite obviously a better drummer than any of the previous incumbents in the group, and began to rehearse with John, Paul, George and Stu in the basement of the Jacaranda. The group were even allowed to play to the coffee bar's customers when the resident steel band had a night off, and evidently demonstrated definite musical improvement in their new circumstances.

It was during this period that the group changed their name yet again. London promoter Larry Parnes had contacted Allan Williams to request that he should hold an audition for local groups with a view to forming a backing band for Billy Fury, who was particularly well-respected in Liverpool. After some thought, Williams decided that four bands should audition for Parnes, one of them (probably the least likely to succeed) being Johnny and the Moondogs. Before the audition took place, it was generally agreed that the group's name was unsuitable, and after some deliberation, it was decided to utilize the same formula adopted by an American star whom the group idolized, Buddy Holly. Holly's

backing group was known as The Crickets, and while considering similar insect-connected titles, someone suggested The Beetles. The quick-witted Lennon immediately altered the spelling to 'Beatles', but few outside the group were impressed, and an initial compromise was Long John and the Silver Beatles, although the 'Long John' part was soon discarded, and for the audition, they called themselves simply the Silver Beatles, a name they stuck with for the remainder of 1959.

It turned out that none of the groups who auditioned that day at a local youth

Above: Erstwhile Beatles manager Allan Williams reflects on what might have been . . . .

John and George with two friends in a primitive attempt to curry favour with a well known brewery . . .

World LP), Harrison, whose idol was rockabilly star Carl Perkins, became Carl Harrison, and Sutcliffe called himself either Stu de Stijl or de Stael, apparently after a painter he admired. Lennon may have adopted the name of Johnny Silver briefly, but it failed to stick and he dropped the idea, while Tommy Moore, perhaps typically, felt that the whole idea of changing his name was a waste of time, and thus could not be bothered to think of an alias.

Allan Williams continued to procure occasional gigs for the Silver Beatles locally, but these seem to have been of little note historically. What was of note was the departure of Tommy Moore, whose injuries incurred during the Scottish tour, added to the pitifully small rewards he received for playing with the band, made it abundantly clear to him that he would be better off returning to drive his fork lift truck, which he did.

Even before they had backed Johnny Gentle, the Silver Beatles had performed from time to time at a Liverpool club known as The Casbah, which was actually the large cellar of a private house belonging to Mona Best, whose elder son, Peter, persuaded his mother to allow him and his friends to refurbish the cellar with a view to using it as a place where they could play records. In the event so many friends congregated there that Mrs. Best decided to turn it into a club selling coffee and refreshments. An obvious added attraction would be a live group. A friend of Pete Best called Ken Browne started a group with Pete, who had ambitions to be a drummer, and The Blackjacks, as they were known, developed into a reasonably major attraction at The Casbah. In the aftermath of their tour of Scotland, the Silver Beatles would go to The Casbah from time to time, and discovered that it had begun to thrive, with the Blackjacks having achieved some local popularity. As luck would have it, Best's group broke up shortly after Pete himself left school during the summer of 1960, which was to prove an interesting coincidence.

Allan Williams, in addition to the Jacaranda, was part-owner of an establishment known as The New Cabaret Artistes Club, which in reality was often used as a strip club, where from time to time the Silver Beatles, for want of anything better to do, would provide musical accompani-

club earned the Parnes seal of approval, although it has also been rumoured that he was not solely looking for a band to back Billy Fury, but additionally for players to back the much less-celebrated Johnny Gentle and Duffy Power, two of his 'stable' who were never destined for stardom. Eventually, Cass and the Casanovas were hired to back Duffy Power on a tour of Scotland. Allan Williams persuaded Parnes to book the Silver Beatles as backing group for Johnny Gentle on a similar tour during May. It was not exactly a taste of stardom, as the accommodation was generally primitive and the van in which they travelled was too small for comfort, in addition to which they were involved in an accident with another car, resulting in Tommy Moore being briefly hospitalized with concussion. Apparently, their money failed to arrive until the very end of the fortnight's tour, which didn't improve matters, but it seems that the Silver Beatles, who had all found it necessary to arrange time off from work, school or college, enjoyed themselves overall, although no more offers of work from Parnes came their way. This was even after they had adopted for the most part new stage names – McCartney chose to call himself Paul Ramon (a name he later used when he co-wrote with Steve Miller in a 1969 song titled *My Dark Hour* which appeared on Miller's *Brave New*

ment to a stripper. The resident band at the Jacaranda was a Caribbean steel band, who were supposedly of better than average ability, but after a German sailor told the owner of a Hamburg night club how proficient and entertaining he found the band the Hamburger enticed them to become the house band at the Kaiserkeller. Allan Williams sensed that if his steel band could find work in Germany, perhaps other more conventional acts would be equally welcome there, and embarked on a pilgrimage to Hamburg to investigate. He enjoyed his trip, and perhaps would have left it at that, had it not been for the fact that he found himself in a seemingly embarrassing situation a little while later. He had acted as intermediary for another Liverpool group called Derry Wilkie and the Seniors who had been booked by Larry Parnes for a summer season in Blackpool, which was cancelled at the last minute, unfortunately after the entire band had given up their day jobs to become professional musicians.

Not surprisingly, they were rather unhappy about being let down at the last moment and prevailed upon Williams to find them some alternative work. In desperation, he agreed to accompany them to London, hoping that he might be able to find them work at the 2Is, which was a coffee bar in London's Soho, a place still recognized as the ultimate rock'n'roll venue in Britain. As luck would have it, another visitor to the 2Is that night was Bruno Koschmider, the proprietor of the Kaiserkeller. Koschmider liked the Seniors, and soon afterwards they became the first Liverpool group to play on the infamous Reeperbahn, the street around which Hamburg's red light district flourished. A little while later, Koschmider wrote to Williams requesting another group, who would play at another Hamburg club, the Indra. Williams' first thought was to send Rory Storm and the Hurricanes, but they were already booked for the summer, while his second choice, Gerry Marsden and the Pacemakers (who would later rival The Beatles in the popularity stakes when the Merseybeat boom became a national phenomenon in Britain) were unwilling to work abroad at the time. Finally, and with some reluctance, since he was a little concerned that he might kill the goose laying the golden egg by such a decision, Allan Williams decided that The

Beatles should be sent out to Hamburg, although they were still short of a full-time drummer. Now that Pete Best was without a group with whom he could make his mark in his chosen profession of 'show business', he was more than pleased to be invited to join The Beatles (the 'Silver' prefix having been dropped earlier in 1960) for their Hamburg residency, although several of the families of the other members of the group were less happy than Pete's mother when they were informed that their offspring intended to work in Hamburg, which had built what can be perceived as a well-deserved reputation as one of the vice capitals of Europe.

During August 1960, The Beatles, along with Allan Williams and his Chinese wife Beryl, her brother and the manager of the New Cabaret Artistes Club set off from Liverpool in a minibus for Newhaven, where they would all board the cross-Channel ferry. A tenth passenger would be collected en route, a bilingual German who was about to start work as an interpreter for Bruno Koschmider. The overloaded minibus was ferried to the Hook of Holland, from where they would drive the approximately 500 kilometres to Hamburg. While the occupants of the minibus were no doubt extremely uncomfortable, five of them at least were very excited at the prospect of their residency in Germany. After all, it was the first time any of them had been to a foreign country.

Rory Storm and the Hurricanes, with Ringo (at front).

From Hamburg to Stardom at Home (1960-1963)

When the Beatles reached Hamburg they were directed to the Kaiserkeller to meet their employer, Bruno Koschmider. While the club was impressive, it wasn't there that they would be playing every night for the next eight weeks, but at a smaller, dirtier club nearby, the Indra. They weren't too concerned about what the club looked like, although they were a little disturbed by their living quarters – a small dirty room with very little furniture situated directly behind the screen of the cinema, which was the building's main function. Nevertheless, after a few days of playing sets lasting four and a half hours, The Beatles were almost glad of the primitive privacy afforded them by the Bambi Kino (as the cinema was called).

Their live show also improved enormously in entertainment value, from an almost static start (no doubt resulting from nervousness) to a point where Koschmider encouraged them to become as extrovert as possible. This approach had additional benefits – at the time The Beatles probably knew between twenty and thirty songs, but faced with having to remain on stage for several hours at a stretch, they had to extend certain songs artificially with long guitar solos and repetition, so that when John Lennon (always the least inhibited member of the group) would jump up and down or roll around the stage, precious minutes would pass. Inevitably, the constant performing also resulted in musical improvement, so that after a few weeks, The Beatles had become a sizeable attraction in their own right.

When The Beatles' engagement at the club ended, Bruno Koschmider decided to move them to the Kaiserkeller even though Rory Storm and the Hurricanes

On the way to Hamburg, the Beatles (minus John Lennon) pose outside Arnhem Military Cemetery. Allan Williams (left), Stu Sutcliffe (wearing sunglasses), Paul McCartney (centre front), George Harrison (second right) and Pete Best (extreme right).

The young Beatles in Hamburg, soon after Ringo joined the group. Left to right, Paul, George, John, Ringo.

were already booked to appear. Koschmider reasoned that if each group played for six hours, alternating on an hourly basis through the night, not only would the club provide twelve hours of non-stop music, but the groups would remain fairly fresh, as they would only be on stage for a comparatively brief period. In practice, this was not the way things worked, as a single hour was too little time for the group that was resting to do anything substantial and most of the breaks were spent topping up alcohol intakes. However, The Beatles also spent a portion of their time off indulging in sexual liaisons, from which there were many to choose in Hamburg. Most of the time, it would seem, nothing of note resulted from these brief encounters, although many years later, in 1983, Paul McCartney submitted to a blood test suggested by a German court in order to establish whether or not he was indeed the father of a girl whose mother claimed to have had a brief affair with Paul which resulted in her birth.

Other than such fleeting relationships, the group kept to themselves for the most part, fraternizing only with the other people who worked at the club and with other musicians from Liverpool who were working in Hamburg, most notably the members of Rory Storm and the Hurricanes, with whom they shared the stage. It was at this point that The Beatles and Ringo Starr began to become aware of each other. According to Philip Norman's 'Shout!', The Beatles, with Ringo replacing Pete Best, actually recorded in a small Hamburg studio as backing group for a member of Rory Storm's band named Lu Walters, who was known by the nickname of Wally. This makeshift group recorded *Fever* and *Summertime*, both evergreen classics, in a studio situated behind a railway station and normally used for recording messages on disc as presents to faraway families. Although four copies of this artefact, which today would be priceless, were made, none of them seems to have survived the passage of time.

It was also during 1960 that The Beatles made their first real German friends, apart from their colleagues at the Kaiserkeller, like the club's chief bouncer, Horst Fascher. Klaus Voorman, a well-brought-up German from a good family, attended a private Art College in Hamburg. Voorman lodged with the parents of another student, an attractive girl named Astrid

Right: A pensive Paul McCartney during the early 1960s.

come with him to the Kaiserkeller, whereupon she was as taken with the Beatles as he had been, but especially with Stu Sutcliffe, with whom she had fallen in love at first sight. Astrid was also very adept at photography, and applied fashionable methods to her numerous studies of the group – the very familiar shot of the group in black and white, with half their faces in shadow, a similar technique to that later used by Robert Freeman for the sleeve shot of *With The Beatles*, was something which Astrid successfully tried in Hamburg. With Stu, she developed a relationship which allowed her to influence her young lover quite strongly in some ways – she restyled his hair, and after initially scoffing, John, Paul and George followed suit, although Pete Best, again showing an independent streak, refused to alter his coiffure. Astrid also began designing and making clothes for Stu, such as a tight black suit, which the others so admired that they ordered inferior copies themselves from a Hamburg cut-price tailor.

In November, 1960, only a few weeks after their first meeting, Stu Sutcliffe and Astrid declared themselves engaged, and bought each other rings. It was obviously a cause for some celebration, but a storm was brewing on a very different front – George Harrison was discovered to be too young under German law to be in a club after midnight, and was ordered to leave Germany. It has never been very clear whether this situation arose because the authorities coincidentally happened to run a spot check, or whether they were alerted by someone. Peter Eckhorn, who managed a new club, the Top Ten, set up as a rival to the Kaiserkeller, had asked The Beatles if they would play there. When Koschmider learnt that The Beatles had visited the new club, and even joined in an on stage jam session, he reminded them of a clause in the contract of their employment that forbade them to play within a certain quite substantial distance of the Kaiserkeller. The Beatles were unimpressed, and actually played for one night at the Top Ten, before George's underage status was revealed, and he was forced to leave the country.

The rest of the group remained at the new club, managing as best they could without their lead guitarist, but as the remaining Beatles moved their belongings

Kirchherr, whose striking good looks were emphasized by her Bohemian choice of clothing. Astrid and Klaus became romantically, as well as socially, entangled, but as with all such relationships, the two would quarrel from time to time. After one disagreement, Klaus wandered around the Reeperbahn. Hearing some loud rock'n'roll music coming from a club, and being passionately fond of rock'n'roll, he went into the Kaiserkeller, where he saw Rory Storm and the Hurricanes on stage. As luck would have it, Klaus sat down near The Beatles, and took in their unsavoury but individualistic appearance before discovering that they too were musicians when they took the stage after the Hurricanes' set ended. Klaus was even more impressed by The Beatles than by Storm's group. On a second trip to the Kaiserkeller, Klaus was determined to talk to The Beatles, and in an attempt to find something of mutual interest, took with him a sleeve he had designed for an instrumental hit record, *Walk Don't Run*.

John Lennon, whom he first approached, was not interested, and directed Klaus towards Stu, the artist of the group, and before long they had become friendly. Eventually, Klaus persuaded Astrid to

Left: Cowboy Beatles in Hamburg, 1960. Left to right, Paul, John, George.

Below: A photocopy of the order from Kaiserkeller owner Bruno Koschmider to The Beatles which forced them to leave Hamburg in late 1960.

out of the Bambi Kino, a small fire started. It was presumed that there was a connection between the group's departure and the fire starting, and Paul McCartney and Pete Best were arrested and jailed for a short time in response to a complaint that they had tried to burn down a club. Eventually, the charges were dropped, but Paul and Pete were also served with deportation orders, and followed George back to England. John and Stu soon found that they had no real alternative other than to return home.

On their unscheduled return to Liverpool The Beatles were somewhat dispirited, and fell out of touch with each other for perhaps two weeks, until they were booked into The Casbah, where, minus Stu Sutcliffe, who didn't contact anyone in the group until several weeks into 1961, The Beatles demonstrated to a hometown crowd that they had improved beyond all measure during their four months in Hamburg. When The Beatles played at Litherland Town Hall near Liverpool just after Christmas, 1960, billed as 'Direct from Hamburg', the group were for the first time adored by a local audience, and were surprised and pleased to discover that girls had even scribbled graffiti on their van.

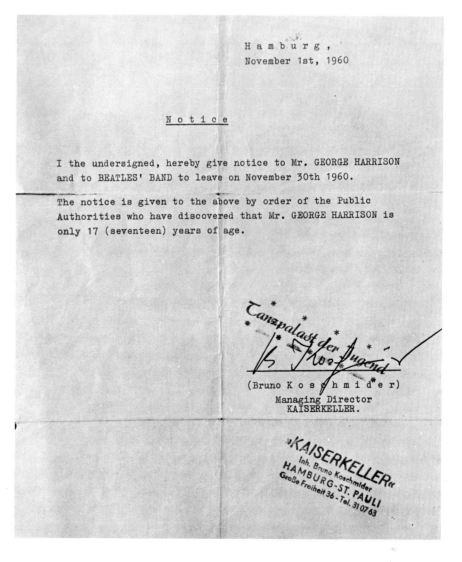

Hamburg,
November 1st, 1960

Notice

I the undersigned, hereby give notice to Mr. GEORGE HARRISON and to BEATLES' BAND to leave on November 30th 1960.

The notice is given to the above by order of the Public Authorities who have discovered that Mr. GEORGE HARRISON is only 17 (seventeen) years of age.

(Bruno Koschmider)
Managing Director
KAISERKELLER.

That concert was also during the brief period when two important new names entered the small circle of 'friends of The Beatles' – Bob Wooler, a local disc jockey with whom the group became very friendly, not only helped them to acquire the Litherland Town Hall date, but also became regular interval attraction at their shows over the following months, when he got the job of resident disc jockey at The Cavern, and Neil Aspinall, an accountancy student, was so captivated by the group's music that he became an unpaid helper with equipment, and would soon travel with the group simply for the joy of hearing them play. Pete Best's mother was

working hard to acquire bookings for the group, and it was through her enthusiasm for the group that they were once again booked to play at The Cavern. Since their previous appearance there, the club had begun to relax its strict 'jazz only' policy, and before long, the proprietor of The Cavern conceived the scheme of presenting lunchtime concerts, drawing on an audience largely composed of office workers. It was a great success, and before long, Bob Wooler had become the resident host at The Cavern, and The Beatles a regular attraction, starting in January, 1961. Incidentally, the girl who looked after the cloakroom was an office worker named Priscilla White, who would eventually achieve her own hit records under the name of Cilla Black.

In April 1961, the group returned to Hamburg to appear at the Top Ten club. By this time, Stu had rejoined the band, although it was becoming clear that not only did Paul seem to resent the bond that existed between Stu and John, but he was also keen to take over playing bass from Sutcliffe, who was largely a passenger in musical terms. Within a few weeks of returning to Hamburg, Paul McCartney took over bass duties when Stu left The Beatles for good to enrol at the Hamburg Art College. When the Beatles returned to England in July 1961, he stayed in Hamburg to resume his studies and continued

Below: On stage at the Liverpool Institute, early 1961 (from left) George, Paul, John, Pete Best.

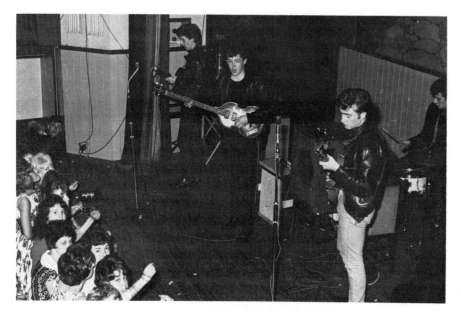

Right: The Beatles with Rory Storm (extreme right) and some fans at The Cavern, August 1961.

to live with Astrid's family. In fact, he was no longer playing with the band when they were invited to make a record – unlike their earlier experiences with recording, on this occasion something concrete would result for The Beatles, although ironically, their name would not appear on the label of the single that was released in Britain at the start of 1962.

A popular West German orchestra leader, Bert Kaempfert, who had experienced an immense world-wide hit record at the start of 1961 with *Wonderland By Night* was employed by Polydor Records in Germany as a record producer and, perhaps in view of his own remarkable success, was allowed to make records with anyone he considered talented. When he saw Tony Sheridan performing at the Top Ten Club – Sheridan and The Beatles were alternating just as The Beatles had alternated at the Kaiserkeller with Rory Storm – the producer signed Sheridan, who nominated The Beatles as his backing group.

Bert Kaempfert was to be responsible for selecting the majority of the material that was recorded. This included a number of songs that were little to do with rock'n'roll, as Kaempfert seemed to feel that at least for a German audience, well-known songs like *My Bonnie Lies Over The Ocean* and *When The Saints Go Marching In,* arranged with

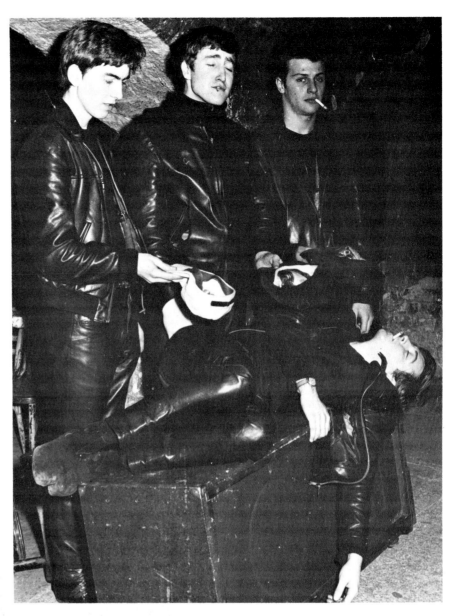

Above: George, John and Pete Best mourn the premature (not to mention exaggerated) death of their bass player Paul at The Cavern in 1961.

Left: Ringo drumming with Rory Storm and the Hurricanes.

Paul singing lead, accompanied by George and John on guitars and Pete Best on drums, on stage in Cheshire, late 1961.

a back beat rhythm, would stand the best chance of success. Among his other choices were *Sweet Georgia Brown* and *Nobody's Child*, the latter performed in the style of Elvis Presley, although he allowed Sheridan to cut one of his own songs, *Why (Can't You Love Me Again)*. Another slightly less obvious choice was a song recorded by bluesman Jimmy Reed, variously known as *If You Love Me Baby* or *Take Out Some Insurance On Me Baby*, while The Beatles themselves were allowed to record two tracks in their own right at the end of the session. *Ain't She Sweet*, featuring John Lennon singing lead, thus became the earliest recording by The Beatles to become a hit, albeit some years later, although it was in fact initially released shortly after *Cry For A Shadow*, an instrumental written by George as a gentle parody of the sound that had made The Shadows, Cliff Richard's backing group, hitmakers in their own right.

Kaempfert considered that a name like The Beatles would be meaningless to German record buyers, and so renamed the group The Beat Brothers. He payed them 300 Deutschmarks each for their day's work (equivalent to about £25 at the time) as a flat fee, with no further royalty payments to be expected. A single containing *My Bonnie* and *The Saints* was released soon afterwards in Germany and apparently sold fairly well. Back in Liverpool at the end of their residency, The Beatles found a few changes – several venues for rock'n'roll (or beat music as it was fashionably known at the time) had sprung up, while an ex-college friend, Bill Harry, was about to start publication of a magazine devoted to the local music scene, 'Mersey Beat'. The first issue of the magazine came out in early July 1961 and contained a humorous account of the history of The Beatles, as written by John Lennon, plus items on Rory Storm and other local acts, including Gerry and the

Pacemakers, who had also been to Hamburg and achieved some success. 'Mersey Beat' would later become a major source of information about Liverpool groups, and an inspiration to those who published their own 'fanzines' in later years. However, despite the obvious upturn in interest in locally produced music, The Beatles found that their financial rewards were still severely limited.

One of the best retail outlets for 'Mersey Beat' was North End Music Stores, a local department store with a flourishing record department run by Brian Epstein, the son of a successful local Jewish family, who had found it hard to discover his niche in life until he persuaded his father to allow him to manage the part of the family business which sold records. Initially, he was dubious about whether he would be able to sell all the dozen copies he had agreed to stock of the first 'Mersey Beat' and he was astonished when they were bought within a few minutes by record buyers desperate to read about local groups, and further supplies also sold quickly. By the time the third issue of the magazine was published, Epstein was himself contributing record reviews. Evidently, Brian Epstein was not an avid reader of 'Mersey Beat' himself, because he was seemingly completely unaware of The Beatles, who were featured quite heavily in early issues of the magazine. Then, on Saturday October 28, 1961, a local teenager named Raymond Jones, whom Epstein regarded as a good customer, asked for a copy of *My Bonnie* by a group called The Beatles. When two more people asked him for the same record within a short time, Epstein knew that he would have to find this potentially big selling record, and began to ask around. He was extremely surprised to learn firstly that The Beatles were a Liverpool group, and secondly that they frequently played at The Cavern which, although he was completely unaware of its existence, was actually little more than a stone's throw away from his shop. Since none of his regular record wholesaling contacts were able to trace *My Bonnie*, Epstein decided that the obvious thing would be to go to The Cavern and ask one of the group which company had released the elusive disc, so one lunchtime a week and a half after Raymond Jones's historic request, Brian ventured with some trepid-

Above: Paul (right) and Pete Best (second right) joking with Emile Ford at the Tower Ballroom in Blackpool.

Left: Bill Harry, founder and editor of 'Mersey Beat'.

Above: George, Paul (looking tired and emotional), John and Pete Best at The Cavern in 1961.

ation into the sweaty atmosphere of The Cavern to watch The Beatles perform, and afterwards approached them to find out which label had released *My Bonnie*. He went back to watch the group several more times, until finally the idea came to him that he might venture into managing them. Meanwhile, he had ordered 200 copies of *My Bonnie* from Polydor in Germany, and sold a reasonable quantity of them.

Being cautious and aware of potential hidden pitfalls, Epstein consulted his family's lawyer and after learning of the previous arrangement with Allan Williams, enquired whether Williams was likely to become an obstacle to his plans. When Williams said that he would certainly erect no barriers to the scheme, Epstein arranged a meeting with The Beatles, to take place in the NEMS offices during the early part of December 1961. Brian Epstein suggested to the group that they needed a manager, and that he would be willing to undertake the task. After an enquiry about whether he would want to make changes in their musical direction

Right: Brian Epstein at the microphone.

brought a negative response, the group agreed to sign a contract making Brian their manager a few days later. Epstein's parents were not wholeheartedly in favour of the arrangement, but Brian assured them that managing the group would take up only a small percentage of his time, and that his main concern would still be the record shop.

He probably sincerely believed that what he was saying was true.

Epstein's early endeavours with the group centred around three areas – first, he decided to formalize their live appearances to ensure that they never played for less than £15 per show, especially as he had agreed with the group to take 25 per cent of their earnings as commission. Secondly, he felt they needed to improve their appearance and their on-stage behaviour, and thirdly, he knew that he must find a record company who would sign them up. This third aim was obviously the most difficult to achieve, and his starting point was a journalist named Tony Barrow, who during a conversation with Epstein mentioned that he had connections with Decca Records, for whom he wrote sleeve notes on a freelance basis. Barrow agreed to mention The

Beatles to Decca's A&R Department. Because Brian ran one of the most successful record emporia in the North of England, this made him someone Decca would not wish to upset, and so Dick Rowe, the head of Decca's A&R department, agreed to send a young man who had recently joined the A&R section, Mike Smith, to see them play.

Epstein was ecstatic that, within a few weeks, he had convinced Decca Records to see The Beatles, and before the end of 1961, Mike Smith had become interested enough in the group to arrange for a formal audition in Decca's West Hampstead recording studios on the first day of the New Year. While Brian Epstein travelled south by train, The Beatles and their equipment were driven to London by Neil Aspinall in unpleasant weather with snow on the roads. The ten-hour journey, which included getting lost in a blizzard in the Midlands, was almost nightmarish. The following morning, the sextet from Liverpool arrived at Decca Studios, but when Mike Smith arrived, he immediately instructed them to forget about using the down-at-heel amplification equipment they had brought with them, as they would work with the studio

Left: Paul and John looking almost unnaturally happy with life.

amps. It wasn't a very good start, and in some ways, the rest of the audition was little better – Brian Epstein was convinced that the best way to impress Mike Smith, and therefore Decca, was to demonstrate The Beatles' ability to interpret familiar material in a fresh and interesting manner, rather than to bombard them with too many original songs. Thus, of the fifteen songs recorded for the Decca audition, only three were Lennon-McCartney compositions, none of which seem to have been re-recorded by The Beatles in later years, although each of them became a hit in Britain when covered by other artists during the early 1960s – *Love Of The Loved* was Cilla Black's first minor hit, *Hello Little Girl* opened fellow Liverpudlians The Fourmost's chart account, and *Like Dreamers Do* was the second hit for Birmingham group The Applejacks.

George, Paul, Pete and John on stage at The Cavern, 1961.

The balance of twelve songs were largely those that the group used in their live show, and covered several different styles – three songs had been recorded by The Coasters, a black vocal group masterminded by white producers Jerry Leiber and Mike Stoller, *Searchin'*, *Three Cool Cats* and *Besame Mucho*, several more were current favourites, like Barrett Strong's *Money*, Bobby Vee's *Take Good Care Of My Baby* and Buddy Holly's *Crying, Waiting, Hoping* while the group's heroes, Chuck Berry and Carl Perkins, were represented respectively by *Memphis* and *Sure To Fall*. Paul McCartney's penchant for what might be termed 'classier' material (a facet which Brian Epstein probably encouraged) provided *Till There Was You* from the stage musical, 'The Music Man', and a cover version of Dinah Washington's *September In The Rain*, both of which were sung in an orthodox manner, which is more than can be said for another evergreen performed that day, *The Sheik Of Araby*, which finds Lennon making strange gurgling noises behind George's lead vocal. Finally, *To Know Him Is To Love Him*, a big 1958 hit for Phil Spector's first group, the Teddy Bears, completed the audition, although the group themselves were unhappy about some of their performances.

Mike Smith, however, seemed quite satisfied, and his enthusiasm convinced everyone that Decca would be in contact to sign them within a few days. What Epstein and The Beatles didn't know was that only one of the two groups auditioning that day could be signed. The other act was Brian Poole and the Tremeloes. Poole's group had one distinct advantage – they came from Dagenham in Essex, considerably closer to London, which would enable Decca to keep an eye on them far more easily. So, despite winning a 'Mersey Beat' poll to discover the most popular group in Liverpool, The Beatles were effectively rejected by Decca. Brian Epstein was allowed to take away a copy of the Decca audition tape with a view to playing it to other record labels but he found little or no interest from other sizeable companies like Philips, Pye, Columbia or His Master's Voice. Brian also discovered that getting live bookings for the group wasn't as simple as he had expected but he was able to advertise them as poll winners and refer to early spring

concerts as 'Prior to a European Tour', because The Beatles were due back in Hamburg in April 1962.

This time, they were due to play at the Star Club, a newly opened establishment where the group would be paid around £40 each per week, roughly 30 per cent more than Peter Eckhorn had offered for a return engagement at the Top Ten. In Hamburg, they hoped to see Stu Sutcliffe and Astrid Kirchherr – Stu had been back to Liverpool for Christmas, when he had looked ill, and had complained of constant headaches and occasional blackouts. Nevertheless, he had returned to Hamburg, but his condition deteriorated and he collapsed on April 10, 1962. He was taken to hospital, but died in Astrid's arms on the way, his death being subsequently diagnosed as caused by physical expansion of the brain. He died on the very day The Beatles were arriving in Hamburg, and they were naturally most upset, although John Lennon, who had been Stu's greatest friend, almost totally supressed his grief, indulging instead in outrageous

behaviour during the group's stint at the Star Club

Back in England, Brian Epstein decided that A&R men might be more impressed if he had the Decca audition recordings on disc rather than tape. After learning that the HMV Record Shop in London's Oxford Street had tape-to-disc transfer facilities, he took the tape there and arranged for a disc copy. The engineer who supervised the transfer was surprised to discover that the tape was far better than most. He advised Brian Epstein to take it to a music publishing company, Ardmore and Beechwood, whose offices were in the same building, and arranged an appointment for Brian with Syd Coleman, who worked for the publishers. Coleman was also impressed, and apart from offering a publishing contract for two of the original songs, asked whether the group were signed to a record company. When he learned that they weren't, he promised to put Epstein in contact with a friend of his named George Martin, who was running the Parlophone label, a minor

A primitive attempt at an early publicity shot?

31

George Martin (second left) gives The Beatles the benefit of his enormous experience in 1963.

small quantities of records, was tied to costs. Even so, Martin was interested enough in The Beatles to agree to them auditioning at EMI's Abbey Road Studio complex on their return from Hamburg. Epstein immediately sent a telegram to the group at the Star Club. On June 6, 1962, The Beatles auditioned for George Martin at Abbey Road and, although he would make no firm commitment to record them at the time, he was not unimpressed. Vocally, he felt that both John and Paul were talented, and he also enjoyed George's guitar playing but, as he made clear to Epstein from the outset, he was unsure about the suitability of Pete Best's drumming, indicating that if he should decide to record the group, he would hire a session musician as drummer.

Coincidentally, both Paul McCartney and George Harrison were also unhappy about Best being in the group. Perhaps, leaving aside musical ability, it was to some extent a social problem, since Pete would not be persuaded to do anything shared by the other three Beatles unless he agreed with it. The additional impetus of George Martin's judgement of his playing finally convinced Brian Epstein to submit to the change. John Lennon does not appear to have taken sides on the personnel change, as he was experiencing very different problems at the time – Cynthia, his girlfriend, had discovered that she was pregnant and John decided that the only decent course of action was to marry her, but the arrangements which had to be made for the wedding, as well as the exciting news that George Martin had indeed agreed to sign them to a recording contract with Parlophone, left little time for something about which he was ambivalent anyway. On August 16, Brian Epstein called Pete Best into his office to tell him that the rest of The Beatles wanted him to be replaced. When 'Mersey Beat' published the news, there was an immediate outcry from Pete Best's fans – many felt him to be their favourite Beatle, because he was more obviously handsome than the others. Eventually, the furore subsided, but the other Beatles and Brian Epstein must have been amazed at the hornets' nest they had uncovered.

Ringo Starr was disturbed too. It was while he was at Butlin's that he was contacted by The Beatles with an offer to join them, and almost simultaneously, he

subsidiary of EMI, whose more powerful labels, HMV and Columbia, had already rejected The Beatles.

Parlophone was very much the poor relation in 1962. It had grown to be a kind of specialist label, releasing records either of strict tempo dance music, or country dance bands, comedy records or LPs of notable stage or television shows. Parlophone had to be self-sufficient, and sales potential, which was usually limited to

Ringo buying popcorn during the early 1960s.

was offered a job with another well-known Liverpool band, Kingsize Taylor and the Dominoes. Had Kingsize equalled or bettered the offer from The Beatles of £25 per week, Ringo might have chosen to join the Dominoes, but as it was, he agreed to become a Beatle and to change his hairstyle and shave off his beard, although he was permitted to retain his long sideburns. He must have wondered whether it might have been better to accept less money and avoid the aggravation caused by Pete Best's fans, but after Brian Epstein contrived to find Best a place in another local group, Lee Curtis and the All Stars, the problems began to diminish.

In the meantime, John Lennon and Cynthia Powell were married on August 23, 1962. There was little time, and less money, available for a honeymoon, so the newly married couple moved into a flat belonging to Brian Epstein. It was

WD 672522

The statutory fee for this certificate is 3s. 9d.
Where a search is necessary to find the entry, a
search fee is payable in addition.

CERTIFIED COPY of an ENTRY OF MARRIAGE
Pursuant to the Marriage Act, 1949

[Printed by authority of the Registrar General

M. Cert.
R.B.D.&M.

Registration District   LIVERPOOL SOUTH

1962 . Marriage solemnized at the Register Office in the
District of   LIVERPOOL SOUTH   in the   COUNTY BOROUGH OF LIVERPOOL   in the

Columns :—	1	2	3	4	5	6	7	8
No.	When married	Name and surname	Age	Condition	Rank or profession	Residence at the time of marriage	Father's name and surname	Rank or profession of father
61	Twenty Third August 1962	John Winston Lennon	21 Years	Bachelor	Musician (Guitar)	251 Menlove Avenue Liverpool 25	Alfred Lennon	Seaman
		Cynthia Powell	22 Years	Spinster	Art Student (School)	93 Garmoyle Road Liverpool 15	Charles Edwin Powell (deceased)	Commercial Traveller

Married in the   Register Office   by licence before me,
by me,

This marriage was solemnized between us, { J.W. Lennon / Cynthia Powell }   in the presence of us, { James Paul McCartney / Marjorie Joyce Powell }   H.E. Sidlmarsh Superintendent Registrar   Eric Welain Registrar

I, ERIC WILLIAMS   Registrar for the District of   LIVERPOOL   , in the   COUNTY BOROUGH OF LIVERPOOL   do hereby certify that this is a true copy of the entry number   61   in the Register Book of Marriages for the said District, and that such Register Book is now legally in my custody.

WITNESS MY HAND this   23rd   day of   August   , 1962   Eric Welain

CAUTION.—Any person who (1) falsifies any of the particulars on this certificate, or (2) uses a falsified certificate as true, knowing it to be false, is liable to prosecution.   Registrar.

Above: John Lennon's first marriage certificate – note the name of the first witness!

Right: The Fab Four on Merseyside on a cold day in 1963.

decided to keep the news that one of the Beatles was married a secret, in case it resulted in the loss of any fans, and the group continued to perform around Merseyside as though nothing had changed. Brian Epstein did manage to acquire several prestigious local bookings for the band, as second on the bill to visiting luminaries like Joe Brown, who had just scored what would be his biggest hit with *A Picture Of You*, and the great American rock'n'roller, Little Richard, although this latter event took place almost exactly a month after The Beatles had made their first recording, produced by George Martin, for Parlophone Records. Among the tracks recorded at Abbey Road studios on September 11, 1962, were *Love Me Do* and *P.S. I Love You*, both Lennon-McCartney compositions, which were released as the first Beatles' single on Parlophone. A body of opinion suggests that the group cut an early version of *Please Please Me* at the same time, although it has never seen the light of day on record. Martin, probably unaware that Pete Best had been replaced by Ringo, had hired session drummer Andy White and although he was still uncertain of Ringo's prowess, he allowed him to play tambourine on *Love Me Do* and maraccas on *P.S. I Love You*, and by the end of the session, perhaps sympathizing with Ringo's difficult position, allowed him to play the drums on one version of *Love Me Do*.

On October 5, 1962, *Love Me Do/P.S. I Love You* was released as the first proper single by The Beatles – *My Bonnie* having neither credited them by name nor featured them as principals. In fact, both versions of *Love Me Do* soon became available – Ringo's drumming can be heard on the initial single release, but when *Love Me Do* was re-pressed around six months later, Andy White's version was used (twenty years later, both versions would appear on the same reissued single). A week after it was released for the first time, the single appeared in the British chart, and slowly limped upwards until by the end of the year it was just inside the Top 20, helped by occasional plays on BBC Radio and Radio Luxembourg – the group had actually made two BBC Radio appearances even before *Love Me Do* was released, and recorded a third session a few days before they had to

return to Hamburg for another two-week residency, which had been arranged some time before.

Brian Epstein, meanwhile, was concerned about the music publishing aspects of his group's career. He apparently felt that much more effort could have been used to push *Love Me Do* higher in the chart through more radio exposure. George Martin suggested finding a small hungry music publishing concern, which would work harder because it needed to be successful to survive.

Above: Windswept Beatles on a pedestal?

John makes Paul a cup of tea without removing the lid of the teapot – magic!

Martin approached an ex-dance band singer turned music publisher named Dick James, but James was not much more impressed than Martin with *Love Me Do*, which both agreed was simply little more than a simple riff given added charm by John Lennon's catchy harmonica playing.

In order to show his good faith, however, and perhaps thereby convince Brian Epstein to allow him to publish future Beatle compositions, he set about finding an ultra-commercial song for the group to record as a follow-up to their small debut hit. A young songwriter named Mitch Murray had come up with a song titled *How Do You Do It?*, which James felt fitted the bill, and George Martin agreed when he heard it. John Lennon and Paul McCartney were considerably less enthusiastic when Martin played it for them, and stated that they would far prefer to record one of their own songs for the second single.

When the group returned to Abbey Road to record again, Martin insisted that they at least attempt *How Do You Do It?*, but The Beatles still argued that one of their own songs, *Please Please Me*, which they had previously recorded at the *Love Me Do* sessions, was far superior. Martin had considered the previously recorded

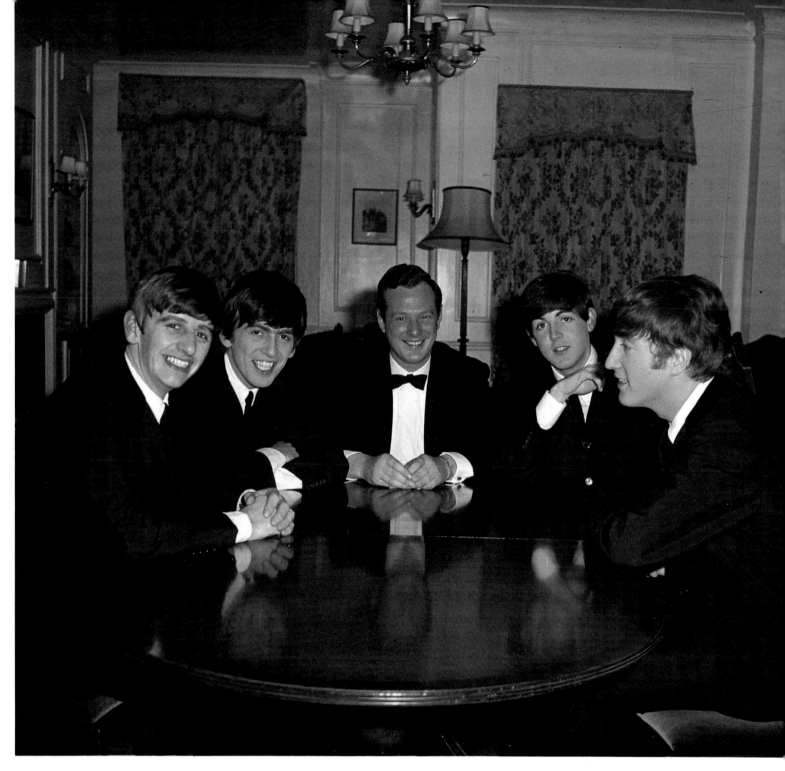

version too slow in tempo and too short, so that when he heard that the group had speeded up their arrangement of the song, he was able to suggest methods of elongating it, and when he was satisfied with a recorded performance of the song, he was sure that it would be a huge hit. He asked James to be allowed to hang on to *How Do You Do It?* for a few weeks in the hope that he could find someone else to record it. For his part, Dick James was less than ecstatic that the song he had suggested was not to be used, but when Martin enthused about the hit potential of *Please Please Me*, James decided to cut his losses and publish the song if Epstein would allow him to. Since Dick James Music seemed to Brian to be 'hungry', he was ready to agree, but in a flash of inspiration, made a condition – if James could provide something special in the way of promotion, he could have publishing rights to the song. Whereupon James called the producer of a pop TV show that had just been launched, 'Thank Your Lucky Stars', played the song to him over the telephone, and received a promise that The Beatles would be booked to appear on the show. Epstein, not unnaturally, was impressed by this instant action, and Dick James had done what would turn out to be one of the best day's work in his life.

Brian Epstein (centre) beams as he sits among his greatest discoveries.

The Glory Years (1963-1965)

The final weeks of 1962 saw The Beatles, with a second single ready for release but not due to emerge until after the New Year, being forced against their will to return to Hamburg to appear for a two-week season at the Star Club. They were particularly unwilling to go as *Love Me Do* was just about to reach its highest chart position, and were even more annoyed to find that they weren't the headlining attraction, that privilege being accorded to Johnny and the Hurricanes, an instrumental group from Ohio who had scored

Slightly apprehensive Beatles pose for a contrived photo. From top, John, George, Paul, Ringo.

several hits (although no one knew at the time that their hitmaking career was over). However, there was another group from Liverpool playing in Hamburg, Kingsize Taylor and the Dominoes, with whom the Beatles spent much of their spare time, and amid the general festivities, Taylor arranged to record several of the bands, including The Beatles, playing in Hamburg, on a domestic tape recorder. On his return to Liverpool, Taylor offered the tapes to Brian Epstein for £20, but the offer was refused. Taylor then passed on the tapes to a Liverpool sound engineer in the hope of getting them released in some form, but nothing occurred until the mid-1970s, when Kingsize retrieved them and offered to sell them to the Beatles for £5000, but this offer was turned down. In mid-1977, after a lengthy process of restoration using modern recording techniques, the tapes were released on various obscure record labels, initially under the title of *The Beatles Live! At The Star Club in Hamburg, Germany, 1962*.

While the performances by the group are not particularly remarkable, largely due to the poor fidelity, a substantial percentage of the twenty six songs included were never officially released by The Beatles, including no less than three Chuck Berry songs, *Sweet Little Sixteen*, *Little Queenie* and *I'm Talking About You*, as well as Buddy Holly's *Reminiscing* and *I Remember You*, a contemporary hit for Frank Ifield, and even two songs on which their old friend, the Kaiserkeller's chief bouncer, Horst Fascher, takes lead vocal. The Beatles had probably forgotten that their rather uninspired performance was being taped so keen were they to get back to England, where they had missed the festive celebrations. Also, they were due to embark on a package tour of Scotland as one of the support acts to teenage prodigy Helen Shapiro shortly after their return from West Germany, although the early dates of the tour found them receiving little acclaim from the audiences, most of whom had evidently paid to see Helen Shapiro.

However, the TV show that Dick James had fixed up for them, 'Thank Your Lucky Stars', was screened in mid-January, and it was at that point that *Please Please Me* was unleashed on the unsuspecting British public, who im-mediately took it to their hearts. Three weeks after it was released, the single reached the Top 20, and three weeks after that, it was at the top of several charts (although the chart which has come to be recognized as the most influential, that published in 'Record Retailer', placed it at Number Two). Not only was the song very memorable, but the image of the group performing it was so different from what was expected – the hair combed forward, collarless jackets and Northern accents, not to mention a left-handed bass

Paul smirks as John and George attempt to stop Ringo leaving the group soon after he joined it.

guitarist whose instrument resembled a violin. Although the population of Britain was unaware of it at the time, they were participating in the start of a phenomenon, and by the end of the Helen Shapiro tour, audiences were applauding as hard for The Beatles as for the headliner.

Meanwhile, on a day off during the Shapiro dates, the group had to spend another day at Abbey Road with George Martin – the somewhat unexpected success of *Please Please Me* meant that an

album was needed to capitalize on the group's popularity, so that in sixteen hours of February 11, 1963, The Beatles recorded ten new tracks, which were added to the four already released on singles to become the *Please Please Me* LP.

George Martin later recalled that due to the speed at which it was necessary to make the album, he decided that the best thing to do would be to use material with which the group were quite familiar as they frequently performed it as part of their stage show. Thus three of the songs recorded a few weeks earlier by Kingsize Taylor also appeared on the group's first EMI album, these being one Lennon-McCartney original, *I Saw Her Standing There*, plus two cover versions, *A Taste Of Honey*, the title song of a stage play, and *Twist and Shout*, a raucous rock'n'roll song which had been an American million seller for a family group from New Jersey, the Isley Brothers, during the previous year. In fact, the LP also included four further cover versions of contemporary American hits, two of which, *Boys* and *Baby It's You*, had been recorded by girl group The Shirelles in 1961, while *Chains*, written by Carole King and her then husband, Gerry Goffin, had been a

Right: The first Beatle LP, originally released in Britain on March 22, 1963.

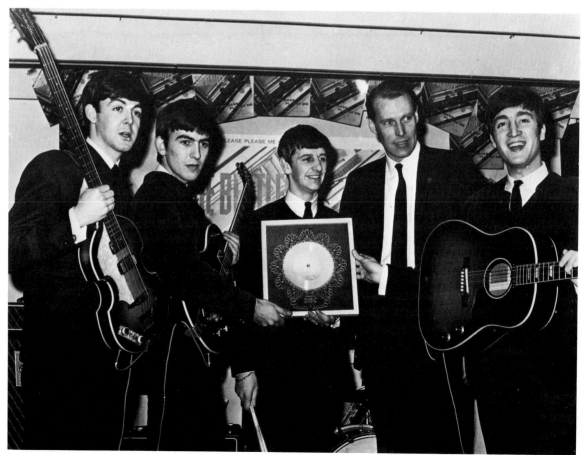

Right: George Martin and The Beatles at the presentation of a silver disc for the Please Please Me *album.*

U.S. Top 20 hit for another girl group, The Cookies. Finally, *Anna (Go To Him)*, a rather less successful song in chart terms, had been written and recorded by soul singer Arthur Alexander. The three remaining songs on the album were Lennon-McCartney originals – *Do You Want To Know A Secret* was used only weeks later by another Liverpool singer who had changed his name from William Ashton to Billy J. Kramer, been signed for management by Brian Epstein and passed on for recording to George Martin, the result being a Top Three hit single, while *Misery* had been written by John and Paul with a view to Helen Shapiro recording it. Unaware of how her hitmaking career might have been transformed – her subsequent hits were very minor – Helen (or her advisers) turned it down, while somewhat surprisingly in view of its quality, the final Beatle original in the LP, *There's A Place*, appears to have rarely been recorded by other artists.

In 1963, the simplest way to record a group like the Beatles on a two-track machine was to separate the instrumental backing on one track, leaving the other for the vocals, the result being that the *Please Please Me* LP was for many years not available in stereo, and when it was re-

The Beatles with a trio of unknown admirers from an older generation.

'I've just dropped half-a-crown there. Can you see it?'

Right: Sleeve for the
second LP, released
exactly eight months
after the first.

With a big hit single behind them, and an album about to be released, The Beatles finished the Helen Shapiro tour and were immediately booked on a similar tour, this time below two American singers, Tommy Roe and Chris Montez, both of whom had recently enjoyed Top Ten hits in Britain, Montez with *Let's Dance* and *Some Kinda Fun* and Roe with *Sheila*. By the end of the tour, audience reaction had made it clear that while Roe and Montez were still major attractions in their own right, it was The Beatles whom most of the punters wanted to see, and they closed the shows with *Twist and Shout* to riotous reaction. Meanwhile, George Martin had been the recipient of yet another act managed by Brian Epstein, Gerry and the Pacemakers, who also came from Liverpool. Martin sensed that they might be the correct group to record the song that the Beatles had rejected, *How Do You Do It*, and it soon became clear that he could hardly have made a better choice when the single topped every major British chart, something that *Please Please Me* had just failed to do. What was most important about the record was that it confirmed the existence of a Liverpool 'sound', which was consolidated when,

leased as such some years later, curious noises were audible on one track in places where there were breaks in the vocals. However, it made little difference when the LP was first released in Britain in late March 1963, and within two weeks it was high in the UK album chart, where it remained for well over a year, reaching Number One in May 1963, and remaining there for more than six months before it was replaced by the second Beatles LP, *With The Beatles*.

Right: Signing
autographs for the pupils
of Stowe School, April
1963.

42

after three weeks at Number One, *How Do You Do It* was supplanted by a new Beatles 45, *From Me To You*, which was in its turn replaced after seven weeks at the top by a second Gerry and the Pacemakers single, *I Like It*. When two other Liverpool based acts, The Searchers and Billy J. Kramer and the Dakotas, also reached Number One during the summer of 1963, it was clear that Merseybeat (as the music was dubbed by the popular press) was the predominant sound of the year.

Amid this great excitement, Cynthia Lennon gave birth to a son, Julian. He was named Julian because it was the nearest boy's name to that of John's mother Julia. Pressure of work added to the fact that the family were about to move into the ground floor of Aunt Mimi's house, made the first few months of Julian Lennon's life a period during which he saw little of his father. An extra problem, at least for Cynthia, was that Brian Epstein had invited John to accompany him on a holiday in Spain – Cynthia no doubt agreed to it because of the obvious pressure on her husband. Some time later, when it became

clear that Epstein was a homosexual who seemingly regarded John Lennon as a potential lover despite his marital status, the absence of the other Beatles would make the apparently innocent holiday a talking point.

The holiday took place in May 1963, coinciding with The Beatles' third single, *From Me To You* reaching Number One, and thus becoming the first unchallenged chart-topping single by the group. Lyrically inspired by the 'readers' letters' column in the 'New Musical Express', which was published under the title *From You To Us*, the song was written during the Helen Shapiro tour by John and Paul at the end of the previous February. If any Beatle record could be said to have been the starting point for all-out fan worship, it was *From Me To You*, which remained at the top for seven weeks before Gerry and the Pacemakers took over, and was also the first of eleven consecutive Number One singles for the Beatles. By the time they were back on tour, this time as headliners, with American heart-throb Roy Orbison as the supporting attraction,

John Lennon with his early trademark black-and-white Rickenbacker guitar.

From Me To You had reached Number One, and before long the Number Two position in the chart would be filled with another Lennon-McCartney song, the already mentioned *Do You Want To Know A Secret* by Billy J. Kramer and the Dakotas. There was now an insatiable demand for Beatle records which was partially relieved by the release of a four-track EP containing tracks from the *Please Please Me* album, but emphasizing the song that was the title track, *Twist And Shout*. So popular was the EP that it finally became the fourth biggest selling record of the year in Britain even though nothing brand new was included on it.

The fourth Beatles single became the quickest thus far to reach the top of the British chart, within about ten days – the more recently adopted practice of selecting a release date to give a record the best chance of entering the chart at Number One had not yet been adopted, or else The Beatles would have achieved this spectacular feat more than the one time (with *Get Back* in 1969) with which they are credited. The song chosen was another Lennon-McCartney original titled *She Loves You*, with a hook line of 'Yeah, yeah, yeah', which would become probably the most recognizable Beatle tag of all time, conjuring up an image of John, Paul

44

and George standing in a line on stage in front of Ringo, who was elevated on a drum riser, and shaking their heads as they stretched for high 'oo' sounds that preceded the chorus. *She Loves You* topped the chart for a month from early September, replacing Billy J. Kramer's *Bad To Me*, yet another Lennon-McCartney composition, at Number One. Curiously, *She Loves You* was finally replaced by a single by the group whom Decca had preferred to The Beatles, Brian Poole and the Tremeloes, whose cover version of the Motown hit, *Do You Love Me*, briefly relaxed the Liverpudlian stranglehold on the Number One slot, but before long, Gerry and the Pacemakers restored the Merseyside domination with their third consecutive Number One (with their first three singles – a feat never equalled), a slightly strange version of

Rodgers & Hammerstein's song from 'Carousel', *You'll Never Walk Alone*, in which Gerry Marsden's quivering voice induced a rather different emotion from that produced by the fun-loving Beatles.

Gerry spent four weeks at the top (and has never returned there since), but after that time, was replaced by *She Loves You*, which resumed its previous position for two more weeks. This remarkable feat, which has rarely, if ever, been equalled, was probably the result of the British media. On October 13, 1963, the group appeared as the stars of a TV show, 'Sunday Night At The London Palladium', which was transmitted live from the famous London theatre. The street where the theatre stands was reportedly jammed with Beatles fans all day, which attracted newspaper reporters who saw at first hand the chaotic scenes the police

Ringo in conversation, 1963.

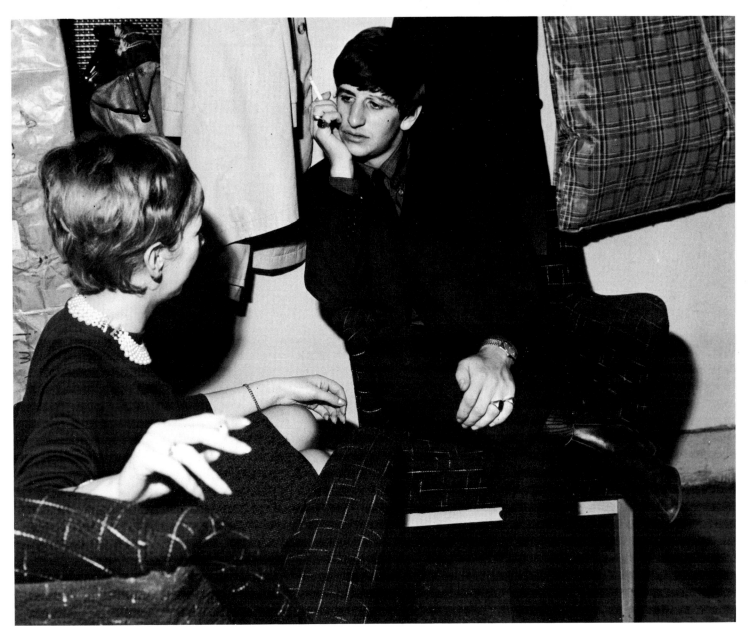

were unable effectively to control. Inevitably, the next day's papers contained huge photographs of The Beatles and their fans and eyewitness accounts of the mayhem, and from that point on, the group, for better or worse, were household names.

The demand for further Beatle products was partially stemmed by the release of two further EPs, one containing the first three hits plus the flip side of *From Me To You* – it would be incorrect to suggest the implied inferiority of the term 'B side' to tracks like *Thank You Girl* or *I'll Get You*, which were released with *From Me To You* and *She Loves You* respectively – and the other with four more tracks from the *Please Please Me* LP. Both sold prodigiously, of course, and by

the end of the year, it was conservatively estimated that the group had sold around seven million records in Britain.

But what of America? Having signed with Parlophone, part of the giant EMI organization, The Beatles were therefore automatically available to Capitol Records, EMI's autonomous American label, although their debut single in the United States had actually been *My Bonnie*, one of the Tony Sheridan recordings, which was released in the first half of 1962 and ignored. With the huge success of their more recent releases in Britain, George Martin offered the hits to Capitol, starting with *Please Please Me*, but was rebuffed with the answer that Capitol felt that The Beatles were not the kind of act that would sell many records in America, a

Grinning George.

Pensive Paul.

reply repeated for *From Me To You* and *She Loves You* in succession. In frustration, Martin contacted a friend in New York and invited him to acquire a deal with some other label. Vee Jay Records, a small but established independent company, were interested enough to release *Please Please Me* and *From Me To You* as singles, as well as a slightly shorter version of the *Please Please Me* LP, retitled *Introducing The Beatles*, but none of the three records made any impact, whereupon *She Loves You* was licensed by another small label, Swan Records, but once again failed to achieve anything significant. It is probably true to say that had either Vee Jay or Swan been prepared to invest more effort in promoting the group, things might have been different, but early releases by the Beatles in the United States seemed to simply confirm that Capitol had been right to reject the group.

Back in England, in the aftermath of the London Palladium experience, fan fervour was notably increasing, particularly after the announcement that The Beatles

Right: Movie star Marlene Dietrich hangs on to Ringo and George at the Royal Variety Performance, November 1963.

Above: Enjoying Royal acclaim at the same show.

had earned the accolade of selection for the Royal Variety Performance, a long-standing charity show attended by members of the Royal Family. Even before the show, which took place on November 4, the riots, which some said had not really occurred outside the London Palladium during the previous month, began in earnest and with great regularity in towns and cities around Britain, but the biggest disturbance came at the end of October, when the group returned from a brief Swedish tour and were greeted at London's Heathrow Airport by literally thousands of screaming fans, who totally ignored two other celebrities also at Heathrow, the British Prime Minister, Sir Alec Douglas-Home, and the newly crowned Miss World. A few days later, at the Royal Variety Performance, The Beatles apparently charmed the Queen Mother and Princess Margaret with their brief spot and John Lennon, introducing *Twist and Shout*, made his much-quoted request for the people in the cheaper seats to clap their hands, 'and all the rest of you if you'll just rattle your jewellery . . .'. When the Royal Party failed to criticize this harmless remark (which the more establishment newspapers perhaps felt deserved condemnation for its lack of respect), the media explosion increased in intensity, culminating in an avalanche of advance orders for the second album by the group, *With The Beatles*, which was certified silver (for sales of over a quarter of a million copies) purely on advance orders.

The album, which again had been completely recorded in a single day four months earlier, was similar to its predecessor in content, including eight originals (but for the first time a song by George, *Don't Bother Me*, alongside seven by John and Paul) and six cover versions. Of the originals, the two most celebrated songs seem to be *All My Loving*, an

Left: Surrounding Millicent Martin at a 1963 luncheon at the Savoy Hotel where the group were presented with a 'Melody Maker' award.

instant classic which was conceived by Paul one morning while he was shaving, and *I Wanna Be Your Man*, which was written for Ringo to sing – he had sung *Boys* on the first LP – but was also donated to the Rolling Stones, whose manager, Andrew Loog Oldham, had briefly worked as publicist for The Beatles. Oldham's group had achieved a minor hit with their first single, *Come On*, but were desperately searching for a suitable follow-up when Oldham met John and Paul and informed them of his predicament, upon which he was supplied with *I Wanna Be Your Man*, which became the first Top Ten hit for the Stones when it was released shortly afterwards. The half-dozen cover versions were dominated by three originating from Motown Records, the influential soul label from Detroit – *Please Mr Postman* by the Marvelettes had been the first American Number One for Motown at the end of 1961 while *Money*, sung by Barrett Strong, had been the label's first million seller in 1960 and *You Really Got A Hold On Me* had been a big hit for its writer, Smokey Robinson, and his group, The Miracles, earlier in 1963. The inevitable Chuck Berry song, *Roll Over Beethoven*, was sung by George, while Paul finally recorded a song he had performed in Hamburg, *Till There Was*

You (which was also one of the songs from the Decca audition). The last of the non-originals, *Devil In Her Heart*, was by far the most obscure, having been a small American hit for a little known group called The Donays in 1962.

The LP immediately went to the top of the British album chart, displacing *Please Please Me*, which had been seemingly immovable at Number One for the previous seven months, and itself remained at the top for around five months – a measure of just how predominant The Beatles had become was that when *With The Beatles* was finally overtaken (in fact, by the first LP by the Rolling Stones), Beatle albums had been at Number One for 51 consecutive weeks. *With The Beatles* also achieved a significant milestone, being the first British LP to sell over a million copies in Britain alone, although this feat was not accomplished until much later, during the final quarter of 1965. Sales were no doubt stimulated by the release, one week after the LP, of a new single, *I Want To Hold Your Hand*, for which there were even more staggering advance orders, amounting to nearly one million just prior to the record's release at the end of November. The song was written by John and Paul in the basement of a house owned by the family of Jane Asher, a young actress who

Opposite: On stage at Finsbury Park Astoria during the Christmas season of 1963/4.

became Paul's steady girlfriend for several years, and with whom he lodged when Brian Epstein and all The Beatles moved to live in London towards the end of 1963. The combined British sales for *She Loves You* and *I Want To Hold Your Hand* during 1963 exceeded two and a half million, and the latter single is said to have eventually become the biggest world-wide seller of any British record at between twelve and fifteen million, but inevitably the phenomenon started in Britain where the single reached Number One at some speed, and held off all comers for five weeks over the Christmas period and for the first two weeks of 1964.

The end of 1963 was a very exciting period – the group were featured on several pop TV shows, being granted the accolade of forming the complete panel of 'Juke Box Jury', a very popular show that featured pop music celebrities evaluating new records, and also headlining the rival 'Thank Your Lucky Stars' Christmas Special. Faithful fans were not forgotten, as the first in a series of Christmas singles (which would appear every year until the end of the decade) was made available to fan club members. There was news of a

projected feature film starring the group, while they also appeared in a Christmas Show at the North London theatre, the Astoria, Finsbury Park – later known as The Rainbow Theatre – for two and a half weeks. But even more significant, although no one knew it at the time, was that finally someone in America was getting interested in the group that had smashed all previous sales records in Britain. Even Capitol Records, after hearing *I Want To Hold Your Hand*, had indicated that they were willing to release it, and a young would-be concert promoter named Sid Bernstein had put his life on the line, financially speaking, by booking Carnegie Hall for a concert by The Beatles in February 1964, although he had contrived to conceal from the management of the famous New York concert hall the fact that The Beatles were a rock'n'roll group. Finally, the great American talent spotter, Ed Sullivan, whose nationally networked television show had first introduced Elvis Presley to America at large, wanted to do the same for The Beatles, of whom he had become aware when he was among the milling throng of fans at London Airport when they returned from Sweden.

Below: The Beatles as the panel of 'Juke Box Jury', late 1963.

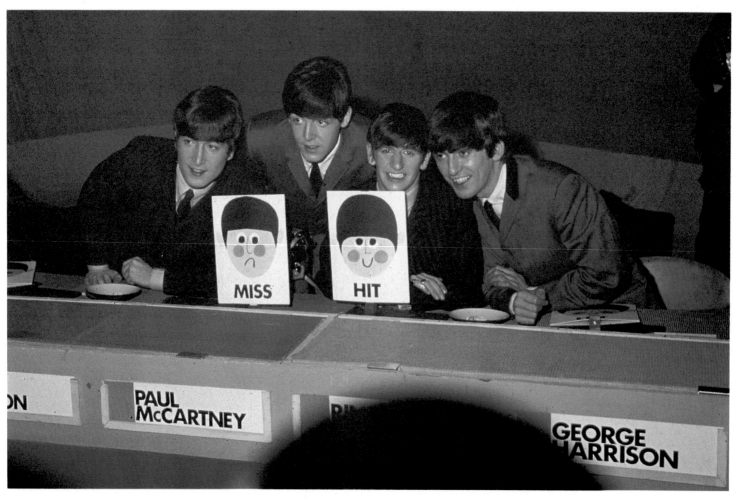

50

Starting in mid-January 1964, The Beatles were undertaking a three-week session at the Paris Olympia, which turned out to be one of their less successful undertakings. During the three weeks, George Martin was to fly across the Channel to supervise German language recordings of *She Loves You* (*Sie Liebt Dich*) and *I Want To Hold Your Hand* (*Komm Gib Mir Deine Hand*), but the group initially refused to co-operate with the plan, for reasons which have never really been explained. However, two days later, as they relaxed at the very smart Hotel Georges Cinq, the news arrived that *I Want To Hold Your Hand*, which had been released in America three weeks before, had moved up the charts at remarkable speed until it was actually Number One – helped no doubt because Capitol Records were finally completely behind The Beatles, in view of the group's imminent American tour. Although this

Paul, as Pyramus, and George, as Moonshine, abuse 'Midsummer Night's Dream' for TV cameras, while Ringo, as Lion, watches between them.

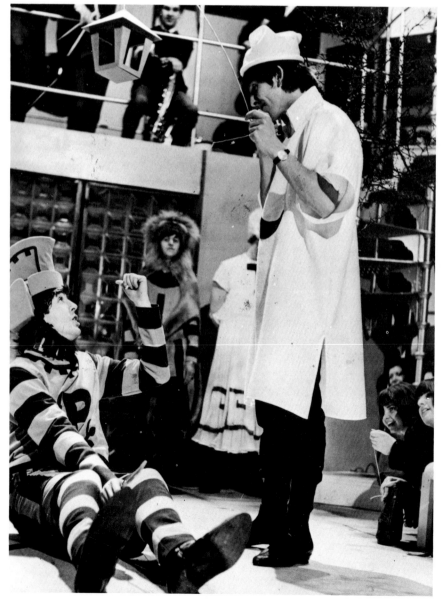

may have been a contributory factor, the manner in which the American public as a whole took The Beatles to their hearts seems to be more connected with the impact of their music in general and *I Want To Hold Your Hand* in particular. Nevertheless, the promotional activities of Capitol Records, who spent $50,000 on their publicity campaign, which involved a nationwide fly posting campaign in addition to information folders and copies of British Beatle records being sent to literally thousands of disc jockeys around the country, should not be undervalued.

The group's arrival at New York's Kennedy Airport was equally well orchestrated – two of the biggest New York radio stations offered a free Beatles T shirt to everyone who went to the airport to meet their plane. The group, along with Brian Epstein, Cynthia Lennon (who by this time was widely known to be John's wife) and American producer Phil Spector, who had become friendly with The Beatles, were seen off by a thousand or more British fans, and unaware of the free T shirt scheme, found five times as many American fans awaiting them when they touched down on American soil in New York. The following day, they appeared on the 'Ed Sullivan' TV show, which was watched by an audience estimated at over seventy million people. Such was the hysteria that the arrival of The Beatles had provoked that even noted religious fanatics were said to have broken their strict rules to refrain from watching television on a Sunday. The handful of concerts played by the group were total sell outs, and the whole of America seemed to have only one subject of conversation, while merchandisers sold hundreds of different Beatle-related items, many of them pirated and of very poor quality – Brian Epstein had tried, at the start of the phenomenon in Britain, to ensure that each item of Beatle merchandise was properly licensed and was good value for money, but the avalanche of applications for licenses forced him to sub-contract this aspect, and even then, the weight of applications made it impossible for proper quality control to be exercised.

On the record front, an enormous amount of activity began to occur. While the success of *I Want To Hold Your Hand* and a Capitol LP titled *Meet The Beatles*

(the equivalent of *With The Beatles*, more or less) could be termed official current releases, and were topping their respective American charts, the earlier recordings licensed to Vee Jay and Swan were vigorously re-promoted to devastating effect. *She Loves You* on Swan rushed up the singles chart and was kept from the Number One position by *I Want To Hold Your Hand*, but eventually displaced it towards the end of March, while Vee Jay, sensing that their opportunity had come, reissued *Introducing The Beatles*, which was kept out of the top position in the album chart by *Meet The Beatles*. They also released a single coupling *Please Please Me* and *From Me To You*, both sides of which made the chart, the former peaking at Number Three and the latter just outside the Top 40, while a few weeks later came an album with the somewhat misleading title of *Jolly What! The Beatles And Frank Ifield On Stage* – the four Beatle tracks were simply the songs from the first two Vee Jay singles that had been unsuccessfully released, while the balance of the record was made up of live recordings by Frank Ifield, who had little or nothing in common with The Beatles. That album just failed to make the Top 100, but a single of *Twist And Shout*, released on a specially created subsidiary label of Vee Jay known as Tollie, was a Number Two hit. Capitol were by this

time screaming for new Beatle product, and actually released the next new Beatles single, *Can't Buy Me Love*, a few days before it came out in Britain. The single effortlessly topped the singles charts on both sides of the Atlantic, and during the week of April 4, 1964, there were twelve Beatles singles in the American Top 100, with *Can't Buy Me Love* at Number One, *Twist And Shout* at Number Two, *She Loves You* at Number Three, *I Want To Hold Your Hand* at Number Four and *Please Please Me* at Number Five, amounting to the greatest ever chart domination by a single act, which is unlikely to be approached, let alone equalled.

At the end of the American tour, which was more successful than anyone could have possibly predicted a few weeks before, The Beatles returned to Britain towards the end of February to complete the tracks that became their sixth single, *Can't Buy Me Love* and *You Can't Do That*, having undertaken the first part of the recordings during their visit to France before going to America. George also celebrated his twenty first birthday, as a result of which his parents' house was crammed with cards and presents that arrived in several mail vans, while John

Lennon had a small book of his poetry and drawings published under the title 'In His Own Write'. It was an immediate best seller, and John was guest of honour at a literary lunch at Foyle's bookshop. Ringo was elected Vice President of Leeds University, and waxwork dummies of each of the four Beatles appeared at Madam Tussaud's. Acclaim was being heaped upon the group from all sides, along with a modicum of 'devil's advocate' criticism, but The Beatles themselves had little time to evaluate the meaning of their situation, as they began their first film at the beginning of March.

A Hard Day's Night – a title which came as a result of a chance remark by Ringo after a long spell of filming – was a film with a script by fellow Liverpudlian Alun Owen which simply portrayed The Beatles being themselves. Inevitably, one of the major selling points was the inclusion of seven new Beatle songs, all written by John and Paul, but as the cinematic industry remained wary of the potential of the group as film stars, the film was shot in black and white. It also marked the point at which George Harrison met his wife to be, Patti Boyd, a model who had a part in the film. Before long, she and George were

Right: A still from the film 'A Hard Day's Night', with Wilfred Brambell (centre).

mutually attracted, and Patti later moved into George's stockbroker belt house in Esher, Surrey, although she and George only formalized their relationship in marriage a year later.

Since there was insufficient new material included in the film's soundtrack for a complete new LP, an EP of three rock'n'roll cover versions plus one Lennon-McCartney original was released as an interim measure in Britain in June 1964, and predictably sold in substantial quantities, although in the United States, two of the tracks were incorporated into *The Beatles Second Album*, a misleading title to describe a record which included odd tracks from the first two British albums which were not included on their American counterparts for reasons apparently connected with music publishing royalty payments, plus previously released singles whose rights had by this time reverted to Capitol. The album joined *Meet The Beatles* and *Introducing The Beatles* at the top of the U.S. LP chart, of course. By the time filming was completed, the demand for concert appearances by The Beatles in most countries throughout the world had forced Brian Epstein to arrange a world tour lasting five months and taking in four continents, and after completing the new recordings which would be included on the *Hard Day's Night* album, but were not part of the film, the quartet prepared to embark for Denmark. At the last minute, Ringo collapsed with tonsilitis, and had to be replaced for the first leg of the tour, covering Europe, the Far East and Australia. The name of his substitute, who was previously virtually unknown, was Jimmy Nicol, reportedly a session musician, who became extremely famous for a few weeks, but on Ringo's recovery and return, which took place in time for a concert at Melbourne, Australia, Nicol reverted to virtual anonymity.

Songs written by The Beatles and recorded by others were still registering in the charts – fellow Liverpudlians Cilla Black, The Fourmost and Billy J. Kramer were still taking advantage of John and Paul's prolific output, and so was a London based duo called Peter and Gordon. Peter's surname was Asher, and he was in fact the brother of Paul's girlfriend, Jane Asher, which led to accusations of string pulling when the first

Above: *John and Cynthia Lennon in 1964 at the Dorchester Hotel for the launch of John's book 'In His Own Write'.*

Left: *Sleeve of* A Hard Day's Night, *the third Beatles LP release in Britain.*

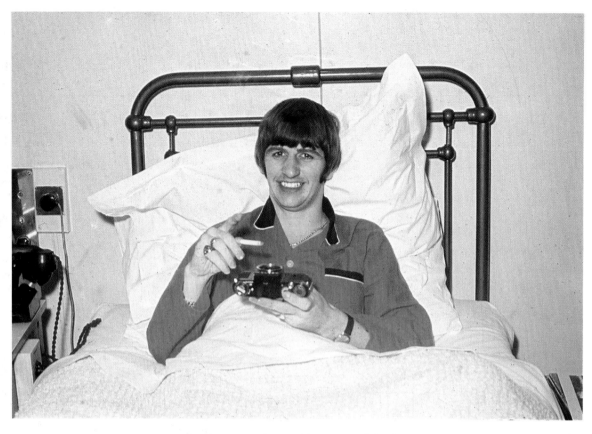

Right: Ringo, now recovered from tonsilitis, proclaims 'I Feel Fine' from his hospital bed, 1964.

Below: During Ringo's absence with tonsilitis, his place at the drums was taken by Jimmy Nicol, pictured here with Paul, John and George.

Lennon-McCartney song recorded by Peter and his partner, *A World Without Love*, topped the British and American charts during the spring, the accusations becoming louder when a follow up, another Beatle song titled *Nobody I Know*, reached the U.K. Top Ten in June, although when a third song credited to Lennon and McCartney (but in fact, like its predecessors, only composed by Paul) was a far smaller hit, the dissenting voices grew quieter. Not that there was time to listen to what anyone was saying, as the group returned briefly to Britain for the London première of 'A Hard Day's Night' on July 6, with Princess Margaret and her husband, Lord Snowdon, guests of honour. The reaction everywhere was predictably ecstatic, and on both sides of the Atlantic, the title song released as a single and the film soundtrack album topped their respective charts, while the film was nominated for two Academy Awards. After a brief period at home, the group returned to their world tour, for a two-month trip around the United States taking in thirty concerts in twenty four North American cities. Record shops were able to reinforce their browsers of Beatle discs with LPs containing interviews with the group, and their concert at the Hollywood Bowl in Los Angeles was taped for a possible live album, although this did not materialize until more than a decade later, which is more than can be said for the literally dozens of bootleg albums, almost invariably of abysmal sound quality, recorded at various concerts on unsuitable equipment and sold cynically at high prices soon afterwards.

Fortunately, things were much better as regards legal releases, although fertile financially oriented minds in America were conceiving bizarre items like a double LP titled *The Beatles Vs. The Four Seasons*, which its sleeve proclaimed as 'The International Battle Of The Century', although what the package actually contained was simply the first Beatles LP as released in America plus an album's worth of tracks by The Four Seasons, who were conveniently also signed to Vee Jay Records. Only eleven days later, exactly the same tracks by The Beatles appeared on another Vee Jay LP, this time under the title of *Songs, Pictures And Stories Of The Fabulous Beatles*, but even these re-

packages appear to have been insufficient to prevent the company going out of business early in 1965. Capitol, meanwhile, released all seven of the tracks included in *A Hard Day's Night* in single form, each of them charting to a greater or lesser extent, and also put together the first of several albums containing tracks that had either been left off earlier releases or were of curiosity value, like *Komm Gib Mir Deine Hand*. Everything (with the exception of some Vee Jay singles which everyone must have already owned anyway) made the charts, although pride of place was eventually reserved for a totally new product in the shape of a single coupling *I Feel Fine* and *She's A Woman*, and the excellent *Beatles For Sale*, arguably the finest LP of the period when The Beatles were an active touring band. At least three classic songs were included, *No Reply*, *I'm A Loser* and *Eight Days A Week*, while the album also contains some of the finest cover versions the group

Below: Puppets on a string? Rehearsing for 'Night Of A Hundred Stars' at the London Palladium, July, 1964.

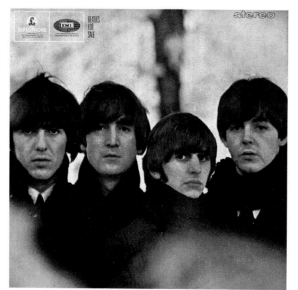

Right: Beatles For Sale, the first Beatles LP of 1965 in Britain.

Right: Help!, *which emerged during the same year.*

would ever record – Chuck Berry's *Rock And Roll Music*, a most pleasing performance of Buddy Holly's *Words Of Love*, a song whose copyright Paul would eventually own when he purchased Holly's song catalogue, and two Carl Perkins songs, of which *Honey Don't*, sung by Ringo, is the more memorable. In typical manner, the LP was far from similar when released in the United States under the title *Beatles '65*, but its fragmentation allowed *Eight Days A Week*, which was not released as a single in Britain, to become the seventh Beatles' single to top the U.S. charts in just over a year.

By the end of what had been an incredible year, during which the group had become the most successful entertainers of all time, the four Beatles found themselves at last back in their own country, where three of them purchased large country houses within a few miles of each other in Surrey's stockbroker belt. Having bought new houses for their parents (or in John's case, Aunt Mimi), George, Ringo and John were encouraged to seek some privacy out of London. As already mentioned, George moved to Esher, and was joined by his girlfriend, Patti, while Ringo bought a house in Weybridge and moved in with his girlfriend, an early fan of the group from their days at the Cavern named Maureen Cox. John and Cynthia Lennon were also

Right: Ringo prepares for a non-existent petrol crisis in the drive of his mansion.

Left: The cast of the 1964/5 Beatles Christmas Show. Billy J. Kramer (between Ringo and George) can be seen, with Rolf Harris and Cilla Black to his left, among members of The Barron Knights, the Dakotas and the Fourmost.

in Weybridge, although their move was somewhat spoiled when John's father, Fred Lennon, made an unscheduled reappearance. Father and son had one meeting as a result of which the former was given a house and a small pension, but when he began to supplement his income by not only selling his story (and what purported to be the story of John's early life) to newspapers and magazines, John made it clear that he would be less than overjoyed if his father ever contacted him again, not perhaps least because of an atrocious single Lennon Senior recorded titled *That's My Life.*

Over the Christmas period of 1964/65, The Beatles again played a season in London, this time at the Hammersmith Odeon, and their records continued to sell in phenomenal quantities. Only Paul McCartney was still living in London, where, it has been suggested, he was playing the part of a socialite to the hilt –

his girlfriend Jane came from a very aristocratic family. In fact, The Beatles were the inspiration behind and the toast of 'Swinging London', and were welcomed wherever they went, as well as being recognized leaders in every field, which sometimes led to less advantageous situations, such as the evening when John and George unknowingly were first given the drug LSD, the effects of which were so little understood that it had yet to be outlawed.

All over London, young people were being introduced to the twin pleasures and horrors of the drug culture, and in this, as in everything else, The Beatles were seen as a litmus test – if they smoked marijuana or took LSD, there were hundreds and thousands of others who might possibly copy them, although there must be doubt as to whether any person, however influential, ought to be blamed for the stupidity of others.

Right: On location for 'Help!' in Austria.

Below: John and Cynthia Lennon about to try their luck on Swiss ski slopes, January 1965.

1965 would see little change in any aspect of the lives of The Beatles, as they struggled to remain at least partially normal while the rest of the world waited with bated breath for their next utterance. The first single of the New Year, *Ticket To Ride*, predictably rose to the top of the world's charts as the first vestige of a second Beatles film. The title of the film was a matter for some conjecture, and in fact the American release of *Ticket To Ride* stated on the record label that the song came from the forthcoming film, 'Eight Arms To Hold You', although the title under which the film was eventually released was 'Help!'. After the box office success of 'A Hard Day's Night', the use of technicolor was no longer barred for financial reasons. On this occasion, a more fanciful plot, concerning the attempts by a sinister gang from Asia to remove a supposedly sacred ring from one of Ringo's fingers, was constructed by a team of scriptwriters, and the lavish production involved filming in Austria and the Bahamas. But once again, it was the seven original songs, this time including one by George, *I Need You*, that gave the film its particular appeal. The title track, *Help!*, is a stunning song, and was released as a single during the week in which the film was premièred, again before Princess Margaret and her husband, who seemed to have become the members of the Royal Family nominated for such occasions.

The single was an almost immediate Number One in Britain and America, while the film soundtrack LP was the subject of enormous advance orders, especially in the United States, where it made history by qualifying for an instant gold disc for sales of over one million copies, something which no other LP had ever achieved.

What the Americans didn't get on the *Help!* album, again for copyright reasons, were the seven songs that formed the second side of the British release, two of which are of special interest, although for very different reasons. *It's Only Love* would later be singled out by John Lennon as perhaps the least favourite song he had written, but Paul's *Yesterday*, on which none of the other Beatles appear – the backing consists of Paul playing acoustic guitar with a string quartet – has become the most covered Beatle song of

Above: At the Press Conference after receiving their M.B.E.'s, October 1965.

Right: Brian Epstein with The Beatles in a dressing room. Ringo wonders if he can manage another cheese sandwich. . . .

Below: Returning from another overseas jaunt (from left in foreground) George, Ringo and his wife Maureen, Cynthia and John Lennon.

all, with a 1975 estimate of nearly 1200 recorded versions, a figure that has undoubtedly increased considerably subsequently. Although it wasn't on the American *Help!* album, it was released as a single in the U.S.A., and during its brief journey to the top of the chart, sold more than one million copies in its first ten days on sale.

'Help!' was by no means the only highlight of the year, however – Ringo and his girlfriend Maureen were married on February 11, and their first child, a boy given the name of Zak, was born seven months later, on September 13, coincidentally the same day that *Yesterday* was released as a single in America. The group as a whole were frequently seen performing, both live and on television, and John Lennon had his second book of poetry, titled 'A Spaniard In The Works', published to enormous acclaim, but the major event of the year must have been the award of M.B.E.s – an abbreviation of Member of (the Order of) the British Empire – to each of The Beatles. It was the perfect seal of approval for the 'Swinging London' set, though a significant number of those previously awarded the M.B.E.

expressed their disgust that four long-haired popular musicians should be admitted to their most exclusive club, and returned their medals, as would John Lennon some years later, although for very different reasons which would reflect even less credit on him than accrued to those who were so annoyed that their decoration had been vilified in 1965.

Before the group were presented to the Queen in October 1965, they undertook riotously successfully tours of Europe, and during the summer, America. The highlight of the American tour was undoubtedly their appearance on August 15 at Shea Stadium in New York before an audience of over 50,000 fans, a show that was filmed, while once again their concert at the Hollywood Bowl was recorded for future use, although the group themselves probably felt that the highlight of the tour was meeting Elvis Presley at his mansion in Bel Air, Los Angeles – Elvis and The Beatles supposedly made music together for some hours, although the absence of any recordings of the event, even on bootleg records, tends to suggest that the jam session which resulted was of little musical note.

Left: Frantic airport scenes as the Fab Four return to Britain in early 1964 after conquering the United States.

The Studio Years (1965-1968)

Right: The Rubber Soul *album, released in Britain at the end of 1965.*

Despite their incredible success and an almost total lack of time to relax, The Beatles were still bound by a contract made some time earlier that required them to produce two completely new albums and two or three new singles each year. This pressure was equally difficult for Brian Epstein and George Martin, as both were not only having to tend to the requirements of The Beatles, but also to look after Gerry and the Pacemakers, Billy J. Kramer and the Dakotas, Cilla Black and also The Fourmost, another Merseyside group under Epstein and Martin. In the year from April 1963, records produced by Martin had topped the U.K. chart for 39 weeks or 75 per cent of the time, a feat that may never be approached. By the late summer of 1965, he had decided to leave EMI to set up his own company.

At the end of 1965, the usual need for new Beatle product was temporarily satisfied by the release of the group's first double A side single, *Day Tripper/We Can Work It Out* – the term indicates that the two sides of the record are considered equally strong, and in this case, John's *Day Tripper*, supposedly a cleverly worded song about drugs, and Paul's somewhat avuncular *We Can Work It Out*, were both requested by record buyers, resulting in the expected immediate Number One hit in Britain, although in the United States, where the charts still reflected the popularity of a song rather than a record, Paul's song topped the chart while John's peaked at Number Five. The single was released on the same day as a new LP, *Rubber Soul*, which contained several songs of particular interest, the most notable probably being another ballad from Paul's pen, *Michelle*, which is supposedly second only

to *Yesterday* as a vehicle for cover versions, having been recorded by over 600 other acts world-wide by 1975. A British cover version by The Overlanders, of whom little was heard subsequently, even took the song to the top of the U.K. charts, while *Girl*, written by John, was also released in two immediate cover versions, both of which reached the British Top 20. Even George's song on the album, *If I Needed Someone*, was a hit by another act, although George himself publicly stated that he didn't like the version The Hollies took into the Top 20 (and since it was their first single to fail to reach the Top Ten in more than two years, The Hollies themselves may not have been overjoyed either). The album also included two songs that have been interpreted as demonstrating how his group's immense popularity was affecting John Lennon – *Nowhere Man* was apparently written about a day when John was sitting in his Weybridge home searching for inspiration that refused to appear. After a lengthy period of frustration he saw himself as achieving nothing and going nowhere – a nowhere man – while *Norwegian Wood* concerned an affair in which he had been involved. Both songs were again chosen by other acts to record, and *Rubber Soul* became celebrated as the first Beatles LP that provided as many as half a dozen songs that others tried to turn into hits.

On exactly the same day as the new single and *Rubber Soul* were released, The Beatles began what would turn out to be their final British tour, although it lasted only ten days. Unlike most acts whose audience tired of them before their taste for touring was exhausted, a process that usually takes around five years, The Beatles were sick of life on the road within a little over half that time, and after the end of 1965, their live appearances were very limited. However, the group managed to keep themselves busy through the early months of 1966 – George and Patti Boyd finally got married on January 21, while Paul, still intending to marry Jane Asher, it was presumed, decided to kill the suggestions that Peter Asher, Jane's brother, was using their special relationship to appropriate potential Lennon-McCartney hits for use by himself and his partner Gordon Waller. After their first two hits with Beatle songs, Peter and Gordon suffered an embarrassing lapse in their British success, although they had several songs in the U.S. charts. At the start of 1966, Paul gave the duo a song titled *Woman*, but asked that it be credited to a non-existent composer with the name of Bernard Webb. It made the charts, but

Above: Bachelor George Harrison and spinster Patti Boyd plight their troth on January 21, 1966.

Left: The certificate to prove it, with George in mid-signature.

Above: John in Commissionaire's garb for a 1966 TV sketch.

from *Help*, *Rubber Soul* and *Revolver*. The bastardized album in question, *Yesterday And Today*, was initially released with what has come to be known as the 'butcher sleeve', but these were quickly withdrawn and the LP resleeved in a more suitable cover, since it was felt that the picture was in marked contrast to the image portrayed by The Beatles of the friendly and homogenous Fab Four moptops from Liverpool. The offending picture was later used on a bootleg with the far more appropriate title of *Casualties*, and the few copies of *Yesterday And Today* which were sold became extremely valuable collector's items among Beatle fans, and have been known to change hands for literally hundreds of pounds.

The 'butcher' LP appeared in America just over a month after the group had played what would turn out to be their final public concert in Britain, as headliners of the 'New Musical Express' Pollwinner's Concert at Wembley Pool, and about three weeks before they embarked on their final world tour, which itself was fraught with problems. After playing for the last time in Germany, where they looked up several old acquaintances from Hamburg days like Astrid Kirchherr and Bert Kaempfert, they flew to Japan for two concerts and from there to the Philippines. Due to a misunderstanding, they failed to attend a large party thrown in their honour by the wife of President Marcos, and local papers accused The Beatles of snubbing their President. They and their entourage were forced to leave Manila hurriedly. It was no surprise that they were not anxious either to tour the world again, or in particular ever return to the Philippines.

Worse was to follow when they reached America in mid-August, still at the peak of their popularity – or so they thought. Back in February, John Lennon had been interviewed for the London 'Evening Standard', and asked his views on organized religion. Lennon's beliefs, allied to his flippancy, led to his being quoted as saying, among other things, that 'The Beatles are more popular than Jesus now'. Britain during the so-called 'Swinging Sixties' found such an assertion hardly worthy of note, but when the interview was reprinted in an American teenage magazine, the off-the-cuff quote was magnified into a headline that was seen as

only the Top 30 in Britain, although it was rather more popular in America, after which Paul confessed to his subterfuge, feeling no doubt that he had proved that Peter and Gordon could now claim that hits were quite possible without using personal connections.

The first single of the New Year, *Paperback Writer*, came in March, but was not quite as immediate a success as the previous seven Beatle singles released in Britain, failing to reach the top position during its first week on release, although it did make it before a second week had elapsed. Nevertheless, along with the news that the group had no immediate intention of touring in Britain, the single's comparative slowness in getting to the top led to suggestions from doubters that the Beatle bubble was about to burst. During the spring, they worked on what would become the next LP, *Revolver*, and shortly before *Paperback Writer* was released, agreed to a bizarre photographic session in which they were pictured wearing white overalls, with pieces of raw meat and dismembered children's dolls strewn about their laps. This was apparently conceived as some kind of joke, and was used in press advertising for *Paperback Writer* in the first instance, and was then adopted in America for the front sleeve photograph of yet another album containing tracks omitted for copyright reasons

Left: On stage in Munich, 1966, during the final tour.

nothing less than sacreligious. Middle-class middle America was somewhat chauvinistically becoming tired of The Beatles and numerous other British groups dominating the lives and conversations of their teenage children, and seemingly had hoped for a change in the situation, although this seemed unlikely as more and more British acts dominated the American charts. Anything from Britain was eagerly accepted, culturally as well as musically, and the fashions and habits of Swinging London were more evident by the day around America. Lennon's chance remark, quoted out of context, was the opportunity for which America's ruling class had been waiting, and starting with a bonfire of Beatle records in the heart of the Bible belt (and coincidentally the centre of the world's country music industry), Nashville, Tennessee, a wave of hysteria spread around America resulting in Beatle paraphernalia being destroyed and a number of radio stations banning Beatle music from the airwaves.

After hearing reports of the furore, Brian Epstein flew to America in advance of the main touring party and tried to defuse the situation, although with little success until it was announced that John Lennon would formally apologize as soon as The Beatles arrived in Chicago. At a press conference held shortly after their plane touched down, John explained that

he was upset by the decline of spiritual values, and his remark was not meant to indicate that the Beatles were in any way superior to Jesus Christ, but that the youth of the era were so little concerned with Christian values that they were more likely to act on chance remarks attributed to the Beatles than in accordance with the Bible. This seemed to appease the American public to a great extent. The tour drew to a close with a final concert at Candlestick Park in San Francisco at the end of August, which would prove to be the final occasion on which the group performed together on stage anywhere.

Above: Crowds waiting outside The Beatles' Munich hotel, just before their concert at the Circus Krone-Bau.

Right: Revolver, *released in the summer of 1966.*

Below: John Lennon as Private Gripweed in 'How I Won The War.'

To coincide with the tour, a new single and album were released. The single was another double A side, coupling a ballad actually co-written by John and Paul, but inclined more to the type of music associated with Paul, *Eleanor Rigby*, with a song that was composed for Ringo to sing, *Yellow Submarine*, whose chorus was soon familiar even to those only just old enough to speak. The single became their eleventh consecutive Number One in Britain, but failed to equal that placing in America, probably due to the 'sacrilege' controversy, which was at its height as the record was released.

The LP *Revolver* performed much more predictably, topping the charts on both sides of the Atlantic at high speed. Once again, the album was plundered by other artists seeking hit songs, although the only cover version that made the British charts at the time was *Got To Get You Into My Life* by Cliff Bennett and the Rebel Rousers, which was produced by Paul McCartney, who had written the song. George Martin feels that the final track on the album, *Tomorrow Never Knows* (originally titled 'The Void' by its writer, John), marked the start of a new era for the group, although it was in fact the first track to be recorded. Its curious effects, produced by John's vocal being relayed through a Leslie speaker, and including a series of tape loops, were certainly the beginning of a period of experimentation in the recording studio that continued almost until the end of the group's career. The luxury of time in which to extend the barriers of the recording process was something The Beatles would enjoy after the hectic years of touring were behind them.

They all found that suddenly they had a great deal of spare time, but John Lennon was the last of the Beatles to jump off the bandwagon, as he was contracted to begin filming as a straight actor in 'How I Won The War', in which he played a minor starring role as Private Gripweed. When it was released in 1967, the film, which also starred Michael Crawford, Lee Montague and Roy Kinnear, was praised by critics, who singled out Lennon for special mentions.

George, meanwhile, had discovered a new and absorbing interest, in Indian music. Earlier in the year, Ravi Shankar, a renowned maestro of the sitar, an Indian instrument not dissimilar to a particularly complicated variant of the guitar, had been invited with another Indian musician, Alla Rakha, who played the tabla, or Indian drum, to George's Esher home, and it had been arranged that after the scheduled concert dates by The Beatles had been completed, George and Patti would holiday in Bombay, during which time he would learn the basics of Indian music and the sitar from Shankar. George had already contributed an Indian-influenced track to *Revolver* titled *Love You To*, which featured a tabla player, and his fascination with anything to do with the Indian sub-continent would later develop almost into an obsession.

Paul was hired to write the music for a film, 'The Family Way', but as the only Beatle who was still unmarried, he found plenty to occupy his mind, largely in the company of Jane Asher, but also, when she was appearing at a theatre outside London, with any number of Swinging London friends. Their relationship, which was presumed by everyone to be heading inexorably towards marriage, seems to have begun to founder around the end of 1966 – Paul apparently wanted a soul mate who lived her life largely through his, like Cynthia and Maureen, who spent all their time tending to the needs of their husbands and children, but Jane, unlike them, had a flourishing career

Below: Paul with Jane Asher, both as part of the audience rather than on stage.

Yoko Ono, pictured during the late 1960s.

grow long after his part as Private Grip-weed, and had taken to wearing wire-rimmed spectacles. His spare time, of which there was suddenly a good deal, was spent in the pursuit of activities that interested him, and one of these was art. From being invited to private showings at London galleries that probably saw him as a rich potential customer, he became very interested in art, and it was at the Indica Gallery in London that he met someone who would change his life. The exhibition on display when John went to the gallery was of work by a Japanese-American woman named Yoko Ono. When she was introduced to John, he was reportedly most impressed when, instead of a conventional greeting, she simply handed him a card upon which the word 'Breathe' was written.

It was perhaps due to George's absence in India that *Revolver* was the only new Beatle LP of 1966, although since they had so much extra time, it should in theory have made fulfilling their con-tractual obligations easier. In America, the problem was less pressing, since the various albums composed of odd tracks, like *Yesterday And Today*, had ensured that a steady stream of 'new' Beatle albums became available – up to and including *Revolver*, there had been no less than eleven original Beatle LPs released (excluding all the repackaging), while in Britain, the total was seven. For the second 1966 LP in Britain, it was decided to collect together the A sides of each single starting with *From Me To You* (and including the two singles with double A sides, both of which were featured) to *Eleanor Rigby* with *Yesterday* and *Mich-elle* plus one track, a cover version of Larry Williams' *Bad Boy*, which had never previously been released in Britain but had appeared in America as an album track during the previous year. In other circumstances, this hit-filled package would have been virtually guaranteed massive success, but since everyone al-ready owned virtually every track on the record, even the fact that it was released shortly before Christmas failed to push it into the Top Five of the U.K. album chart.

However, during December 1966, the group assembled at Abbey Road studios to begin work on what was destined to be their most influential album, beginning

of her own that had nothing to do with The Beatles, and from that point of view, possessed an independence Paul found difficult to comprehend. Wasn't it true that wherever The Beatles went, they were treated like royalty? How could it be, then, that Jane preferred to work in reper-tory somewhere miles from London to being with him? Paul even wrote a song about his feelings, which appeared on the *Rubber Soul* album, *I'm Looking Through You*, but Jane refused to be drawn.

Of the four Beatles, Ringo's life was probably the least complicated, which may be seen as a very positive reflection on his attitude to such matters. George was away in India, but John found sitting at home in Weybridge less stimulating than Ringo – he had not allowed his hair to with work on two songs written by Paul, *Penny Lane* and *When I'm 64*. The former referred to an actual part of Liverpool, and the latter was also connected with the group's early days, as Paul had begun to write it while the group were still resident at The Cavern. Another December session saw work on a song of John's, also about a part of Liverpool, *Strawberry Fields Forever*, although neither *Penny Lane* nor *Strawberry Fields* would actually appear on the album, *Sergeant Pepper's Lonely Hearts Club Band*, when it was finally released six months later. Instead, they were released during February 1967 as a double A sided single and, remarkably, failed to reach Number One in Britain, being held back in second place by the totally retrogressive *Release Me*, a sickly ballad performed by a previously unsuccessful ex-dance band singer named Arnold Dorsey, who had been specially re-christened professionally with the name Engelbert Humperdinck. There was no such problem in the United States, where advance orders for the single topped a million copies, and *Penny Lane* topped the charts while *Strawberry Fields* was close behind at Number Five.

The single's failure to reach the top position was ironic in view of the fact that it was the first record by The Beatles to benefit from a much improved royalty arrangement that finally replaced their original contract, which had been in operation since *Love Me Do* and had generated huge profits for EMI. From a musical viewpoint, it is also curious in retrospect that British record buyers were comparatively diffident, as *Strawberry Fields*, in particular, is seen as a remarkable piece of work, especially considering that the single is actually two recordings of the same song recorded separately in different keys and at different tempi, John Lennon having decided after two attempts that he wanted to use the first half of the first attempt and the final part of the second, and leaving George Martin to perform the difficult task of splicing the two quite different sections together without the join being noticeable. Meanwhile, recording for the projected LP continued throughout the early months of the year, and during January, Brian Epstein merged his company, NEMS Enterprises, with another company headed by an Australian, Robert Stigwood, who already

Neil Aspinall, long-time Beatle associate, who became a director of Apple.

managed an exciting new trio known as Cream which included guitarist Eric Clapton, a great friend of George Harrison, and was about to unleash another group, The Bee Gees, in Britain. Epstein also purchased his own country house in Sussex, and The Beatles formed their own company, Apple, whose aim was to encourage and patronize any enterprise which one or more of them felt was deserving, encompassing records, films, writers and even inventors. The idea of presiding over an empire of creative people whom they would finance initially until profits were made, which could then be ploughed back into further worthy causes, was greatly appealing.

For the first time, the group were able to spend as long as they wanted in the recording studio without being limited by the pressures of previously arranged concert tours. It was a freedom they greatly enjoyed, particularly John and Paul, and the new LP took nearly four months to complete. It was Paul's idea that the album should have a concept of sorts, which he saw as a kind of variety show in which a unifying factor was Sergeant Pepper's Lonely Hearts Club Band, and instead of the usual strip of silent vinyl between each track, each one should run into the next to create the impression of a live concert where one act follows another without a break. However, these aspects were comparatively simple compared with some of the other problems with which George Martin had to cope – on a song titled *Being For The Benefit Of Mr Kite*, John Lennon decided that he needed a sound such as that produced by an old-fashioned steam organ, and Martin was

forced to improvise by using a recording of a fairground organ playing *Stars And Stripes Forever*, which he taped, then cut the tape into small pieces and jumbled up before sticking the pieces together in random order. The final track on the LP, *A Day In The Life*, is generally regarded as the last song on which John Lennon and Paul McCartney actively collaborated, although all their songs recorded by The Beatles or other artists up to this point and for some time hence was credited to 'Lennon-McCartney', despite the fact that many of the songs were composed individually by one or the other. *A Day In The Life* supposedly came about when John Lennon began to write lyrics inspired by items in a daily paper.

When John had exhausted these possibilities, Paul suggested incorporating parts of a new song he had started to write, beginning 'Woke up, Fell out of bed', but

the song seemed to Martin to contain large gaps which he felt should be filled. Paul decided that what was required was a symphony orchestra who should be instructed to 'freak out', but since it seemed to Martin unlikely that trained classical musicians would be prepared to play in such a manner, if indeed they had any idea what was meant by 'freaking out', he wrote a musical score for the orchestra, who were also required to create a climax to the song by building to an enormous crescendo. To achieve this, Martin wrote a separate score for each instrument, which started with the lowest and ended with the highest note in each instrument's range, together with the instruction to perform the music 'poco a poco gliss', which means (more or less) 'slide gently upward'. As a final touch, The Beatles invited many of their friends to attend the orchestral session, and convinced the

members of the orchestra to wear party hats and false noses.

The Beatles must have felt that the completed album was something rather special (although there were obvious reservations about George's *Within You, Without You*, a droning five-minute long Indian piece which ends with a burst of laughter – this was not, as popularly supposed, the other Beatles laughing with relief that the song had finished, but George's idea for the best way to return to the overall light-hearted vein of the album after his solemn interlude), and wanted the packaging to reflect the extraordinary qualities which they felt the music contained. One rather pointless example which can be found on the record comes in the 'run out' groove of side two, which contains a high frequency note inaudible to the human ear, but which can be heard by dogs, followed by a snippet of distorted and almost incomprehensible conversation which appears to say different things when played forwards and then backwards.

This presumably harmless gimmickry was relatively simple to achieve, which is more than can be said of the album's sleeve – a full-colour montage of pictures of 57 people the Beatles supposedly admired, ranging from obvious heroes like Mae West, Fred Astaire and Bob Dylan to more controversial choices like occultist Aleister Crowley, Karl Marx and Liverpool footballer Albert Stubbins. The onerous task of getting permission from each of these personalities was given to Brian Epstein's personal assistant who endeavoured to contact everyone alive

within the week she was allotted. As well as an insert sheet of cut-outs (of a false moustache and 'sergeant's stripes', etc.), it was decided that the lyrics to each of the thirteen songs – the title track was briefly reprised – should be printed on the rear of the sleeve, which seems to have been the first time this had happened, and was a pioneering move that would be widely copied.

All in all, *Sergeant Pepper* was the crowning jewel in the year of 1967, which was later termed 'The Summer of Love', not least because during the same month in which the LP was released (and immediately topped the British charts for just under six months, and was at Number One in America for nearly four months – and also won four Grammy Awards), The Beatles participated in the first live TV show, titled 'Our World', screened all over the world simultaneously via a satellite link-up. Reportedly viewed by several hundred million people in 24 countries, the group were seen apparently recording their new single, *All You Need Is Love* before the cameras, although what actually happened was that the group added live vocals to an already prepared backing track. Unsurprisingly, the resulting single was a monster hit around the world.

Life was less of a joy, however, for one person who was a major part of the group's success story. With the end of the touring era, Brian Epstein found that he was becoming increasingly distanced from the group, and although he tried to find substitutes, such as his purchase of the Saville Theatre, where he presented some of the finest pop concerts ever seen in London, he had become increasingly reliant on drugs. He was also, although this would not become clear except to his closest friends until later, an active homosexual. He was, according to those who associated with him at the time, deeply unhappy, which led to erratic behaviour, although in between his almost constant use of drugs would briefly revert to some kind of normality.

When Paul McCartney admitted taking LSD in an interview, Brian backed him up by saying that he too had 'taken a trip', although it has been suggested that this support was to some extent motivated by Epstein's fear that his contract with The Beatles, which expired in October, 1967, might not be renewed. Whether this fear

Perhaps the finest and most enduring LP of the 1960s, the remarkable Sergeant Pepper's Lonely Hearts Club Band.

was justified, we shall never know. The Beatles had found a new interest, to which they were introduced by Patti Harrison, who had come across one of the followers of an Indian guru known as the Maharishi Mahesh Yogi. Patti was impressed by what she believed the Maharishi represented and of course told George about it, and when it was discovered that the Indian gentleman would be giving a lecture in London during August 1967, Patti's enthusiasm was enough to persuade all the Beatles to attend. They were most impressed by the Maharishi, who offered peace through his mystical meditation exercises, plus a greater awareness and happiness, and after the lecture, each of them decided to become followers. They were then invited to a summer school due to start the following day in Bangor, North Wales. Brian Epstein was invited to accompany the party of travellers who took the train to Wales, but since a Bank Holiday weekend was approaching, he declined the offer as he had made other arrangements.

The media had been alerted to this semi-public appearance by the always newsworthy Beatles, and were waiting in Bangor when the trainload of meditators arrived. The following day, news came that deflated the euphoria the quartet and their ladies were feeling – Brian Epstein was dead! The circumstances of his death are curious – in simple terms, he had

Top: On location during the filming of 'Magical Mystery Tour', John and George (left) and Paul (third right) buying fish and chips.

Above: Paul signing autographs on the beach at Newquay in Cornwall during the 'Magical Mystery Tour' excursion.

already befuddled mind having forgotten that he had already taken a substantial dose of a sleeping drug.

The Beatles were informed by telephone of Brian's death and returned to London before the end of the ten-day course, as a great many business matters needed attention – Brian Epstein's brother, Clive, became the new head of NEMS, but The Beatles decided that from that point on, they would not be requiring a manager, as such. After all, they would no longer be touring, and they could look after Apple themselves, while the next major project, a TV film with (of course) some Beatle music titled 'Magical Mystery Tour', was already well into the planning stages. When they undertook their next project they began to quickly realize how important Brian had been. Once again, the initial idea was Paul's, although the title song was actually written during the sessions for *Sergeant Pepper*, but had been largely forgotten in the wake of that album's release, the satellite TV show, the Maharishi and Brian's death. When the group returned to comparative normality, they remembered the song, and it became central to the idea conceived by Paul, which was to hire a coach in which the group would travel and film its progress on a real mystery tour around England. Perhaps more important, they would direct the film themselves. So excited were the group by this prospect that they decided to postpone a projected trip to India to see the Maharishi until the following year.

The early part of September 1967, was spent recording new songs to be incorporated into the project, and on the eleventh of the month, the 'Magical Mystery Tour' actually started. With remarkable naïveté, no one had foreseen that the coach containing the group and the actors and film crew they had engaged would be followed everywhere by a possee of pressmen, eager to report on this new venture. It also became dramatically clear that without Brian Epstein's organizational experience, apparently simple matters like finding accommodation were far from straightforward. Eventually, after two days during which they caused chaos on the roads of Britain, the coach was abandoned and more filming was undertaken on a disused airfield in Kent, after which an even more chaotic period of editing

intended to host a party at his recently acquired country house in Sussex, but several of the expected guests had not arrived, so Brian had driven back to London leaving the only two guests still at the party by themselves. Both the guests, Peter Brown and Geoffrey Ellis, were old friends and trusted business partners, and were apparently quite used to such odd behaviour. Brian spoke to them during the next day, and arranged to return to Sussex, but it was a journey which he didn't make – when the staff at his London home heard nothing of him for a period of many hours, a doctor was called, and Brian was found to be dead. While he was widely presumed to have committed suicide, a perhaps more credible theory is that he accidentally took an overdose of one of the many 'medications' he used, his

occurred, with each Beatle altering what another member of the group had decided was to be the final composition of the film. Fortunately, during this period, a new single was recorded and released in late November, and restored the impetus that had begun to dissipate during the filming. The song was *Hello Goodbye*, and after the curious comparative failure of *Strawberry Fields/Penny Lane*, restored the group's slightly battered confidence by topping the charts in both Britain and America, while a song from the film's soundtrack, *I Am The Walrus*, provided a trailer for 'Magical Mystery Tour' on the single's B side.

Perhaps the only problem caused by *Hello Goodbye* was that it prevented the soundtrack recordings from 'Magical Mystery Tour' (released in Britain in the

form of two EP records in a special sleeve containing a 24-page booklet) from topping the British charts when it was released two weeks afterwards. Although the film itself had been made in colour, the decision was made to sell it to BBC Television, who had only begun colour transmission a short time before, as a result of which few colour TV sets were owned in Britain. The BBC decided, amid many fanfares, to screen the film on Boxing Day, when it was certain that a huge audience would be watching. Unfortunately, the lack of colour, together with the confused nature of the film – no script was prepared, the intention being that a kind of 'cinéma-vérité' technique would result in some kind of plot occurring organically – led to enormous disapproval of the end result on the part of the

Above: Paul standing by the coach which carried the Magical Mystery Touring party.

critics. On the other hand the silent millions who watched it seemed to enjoy most of the music, but were completely taken aback by the lack of discernible plot, although many refused to air their views in case they had somehow missed something that was blatantly obvious. It was The Beatles, after all, and they didn't do things for no reason, did they?

There were other matters that needed the attention of The Beatles in late 1967, before the unveiling of their film. Ringo had been signed to make his first film without the rest of the group. It was a cinematic version of American novelist Terry Southern's erotic book 'Candy' in which Ringo played the fairly minor part of a Mexican gardener alongside a galaxy of acting talent that included Richard Burton, Marlon Brando, James Coburn and Walter Matthau. The finished movie was regarded as disappointing, although it can have done little harm to Ringo's acting ambitions. At the same time as Ringo was starting filming, one of the earliest Apple enterprises, a boutique in London's fashionable Baker Street, was opened. An old school chum of John Lennon's, Pete Shotton, was persuaded to manage the shop, while a good deal of the stock was designed by a group of neo-hippies, most of whom came from Holland, and were collectively known as 'The Fool'. They had designed costumes for The Beatles' TV performance of *All You Need Is Love*, and were regarded in fashion circles as heralds of styles that would become trendy in the rest of the decade. The Beatles commissioned The Fool to design the Apple boutique, and to supply the clothes that would be sold inside. They began by transforming what had been an ordinary building, with little on the surface to distinguish it from its neighbours, into a garish psychedelic structure which could be seen from a considerable distance away. Another supplier was a Greek inventor known as 'Magic Alex', one of whose products, a box with bulbs which would light up in no discernible sequence, had greatly impressed John Lennon – Alex was involved with the interior lighting of the boutique. When it opened, it was a sensation, but it soon became clear that in their desire to create a shop that was quite different from all other shops, The Beatles and The Fool had completely neglected to ensure that normal retail precautions against shoplifting had been taken, and before long, numerous 'cus-

Right: A sinister Ringo as the Mexican gardener in his first film without the other Beatles, 'Candy'.

Opposite: The exterior of Apple boutique in Baker Street. It was no great surprise that the neighbours were unhappy!

Right: Rita Tushingham (centre) listens while fellow thespian Michael York attempts She Loves You on a sitar. George (left) looks faintly amused.

Right: The Beatles and other showbiz disciples of the Maharishi pose before the master on his throne.

tomers' were helping themselves to whatever they could remove without detection. After the boutique, other Apple enterprises began to spring up – an electronics division run by Magic Alex, Apple Films, whose first product was 'Magical Mystery Tour'; Apple Records, one of whose executives was Peter Asher, Jane's brother, who by this time had abandoned his own performing career; and Apple Publicity, which was overseen by Derek Taylor, who had worked for Brian Epstein before leaving to become a media personality in Hollywood, but returned when The Beatles offered him a new job.

Even before The Beatles and their escorts travelled to India in mid-February in 1968 for their postponed visit to the Marahishi, things were appearing to get out of hand at the boutique. By the end of July, that particular dream was over, as the boutique's staff were given redundancy notices, and the entire stock of the shop was given away, but before that had come the trip to India, originally scheduled for three months. Ringo and

Maureen stayed for only ten days, the drummer claiming that he found Indian food not to his taste, and that he missed his son Zak. The remaining members of the group, plus Beach Boy Mike Love, Donovan and Mia Farrow, had more stamina, although Paul and Jane Asher returned to England after six weeks, claiming that they had recharged their creative batteries, and wanted to get back to normality. John and George and their wives stayed for nearly ten weeks, but eventually, John informed the guru that they were leaving. When the Maharishi asked why, John replied: 'You know everything, so you should be able to work it out for yourself'. Subsequently, the group admitted that they were probably wrong to have become so deeply involved although George continued to be deeply interested in other aspects of Indian culture, notably Indian music. To tide them over the expected three months away from home, The Beatles had released a new single, *Lady Madonna*, the B side of which was in fact the first song written by George to appear on a single by The Beatles in Britain, *The Inner Light*, Ringo seems not to have participated at all in its recording, while John and Paul were only marginally involved in the supply of vocal harmonies, the bulk of the track featuring George directing a group of Indian musicians, over whose backing he added a lead vocal. Unsurprisingly, *Lady Madonna*, written by Paul, was far more popular. Paul sang lead and played piano in a manner somewhat similar to the way it was played on a single produced by George Martin a decade earlier, *Bad Penny Blues* by Humphrey Lyttleton and his band. On this occasion, *Lady Madonna* failed to reach Number One in the United States, although it did sell a million copies within a week, and was at the top of the British charts within two weeks of release.

Meanwhile, non-group activities included George Harrison agreeing to write and record music for the soundtrack of a rather obscure film, 'Wonderwall', while Paul produced an album for his brother and another member of Scaffold, 'McGough & McGear', and the first acts were signed by Apple Records, in the shape of Grapefruit and a Welsh band originally called The Iveys, but later better known as Badfinger. A girl who also came from Wales, named Mary Hopkin, created a stir by winning a TV talent contest for several weeks in a row, and Twiggy, one of the most famous fashion models in the world, suggested to Paul that she would be worth signing to Apple Records. Paul also spent time in New York with John, the reason for the trip being to announce the formation of Apple and launch the company in America, and during the brief visit Paul became attracted to a lady photographer named Linda Eastman, although he was still engaged to Jane Asher. During the same month, John's friendship with Yoko Ono blossomed, and during one night in May 1968, he and Yoko recorded an album which could be termed experimental, but which many people failed to understand. Cynthia was away on holiday with Patti Harrison's sister, Jenny Boyd (about whom Donovan wrote the song

Below: Disc jockey Pete Brady listens as Paul and Mary Hopkin rehearse a new song.

Right: Paul muses while Linda Eastman (later his wife, but then a photographer) inspects his upper lip after the removal of his facial hair.

Below: Paul (centre) holds Julian Lennon's hand before crossing the road with Jane Asher.

Jennifer Juniper, as she ran a market stall named Juniper), and John and Yoko had the Weybridge mansion to themselves, and cemented their intense friendship by recording the album and making love.

During this period, the group were assembling from time to time to record new tracks for the next LP and a new single. The latter, *Hey Jude*, was featured a few days after it was released in a TV show hosted by David Frost, and despite its length – it is seven and a quarter minutes long – it topped the charts in Britain and America, providing the Apple label with a Number One hit with its first release. In Britain it was knocked off the top of the chart by the second Apple release, *Those Were The Days*, sung by Mary Hopkin, the Welsh girl whom Twiggy had recommended to Paul, who himself produced the record. Even so, the new Beatles album was taking a long time to record, and during the five months spent in recording it, George Martin went on holiday, leaving his assistant, Chris Thomas, today a notable producer but in 1968 a virtual novice, to do what he could to help out. Thomas was naturally enormously overawed, although he eventually contributed as engineer/producer of eight songs, as well as playing keyboards on a couple of tracks, and recalls that from time to time, the group would call a halt to recording and have lengthy discussions among themselves concerning Apple and

Left: Apple executives around their first hitmaker, Mary Hopkin. Derek Taylor (left), Peter Asher (seated on floor), Tony Bramwell (squatting) and Ron Kass.

what should be done with it. A further problem was a commitment to compose some new material for the soundtrack of a cartoon feature in which animated versions of the four Beatles starred, 'Yellow Submarine', but fortunately, the long stay in India had given each of the group, including even Ringo, the opportunity to write a number of new songs. It soon became clear that the new album could turn out to be a double LP, so much material was available, and its eventual release as such to some extent justified the length of time spent recording it. Another innovation – this was the first two-record set released by The Beatles – was the sleeve. After seeing a collage prepared by a designer named Richard Hamilton on the subject of their friends and rivals, the Rolling Stones, Paul invited Hamilton to submit a design for the new LP. Hamilton, however, said that he was not prepared to add to the vast number of garish sleeve designs that were the order of the

Right, and on following three pages: The colour prints of the four Beatles given away with The Beatles, *the so called 'double white' album. (This page) John Lennon.*

day, and in an inspired moment, suggested that the sleeve should be plain white laminated board, with perhaps the group's name, still in white, embossed on it, the only other decoration being a number stamped on each sleeve to give the impression that it was a limited edition. As an additional feature, he suggested that the group themselves create a collage that could be enclosed with the album in the form of a poster. These revolutionary ideas were eagerly accepted by the group, who also provided individual full-colour pictures of themselves in the package, and printed the lyrics to all thirty tracks on the back of the poster.

Simply titled *The Beatles*, the double album was released to huge acclaim in late November 1968, and for many years was the biggest selling double LP of all time,

Ringo Starr.

although it has more recently been overtaken by the soundtrack to the film 'Saturday Night Fever'. However, a year later, the album would become controversial for a very different and most unsavoury reason, when mass murderer Charles Manson suggested that he and his band of followers had used the songs on the records, notably *Helter Skelter*, *Rocky Raccoon*, *Piggies* and *Happiness Is A Warm Gun*, as a blue print for the otherwise completely motiveless killing of several people, including American film star Sharon Tate. Another track on the album, *Sexy Sadie*, was written by John, while *Dear Prudence* is dedicated to Mia Farrow's sister, and *Back In The U.S.S.R.* was designed as a pastiche of the style of the Beatles' main American rivals, the Beach Boys. Ringo contributed his first

Paul McCartney.

song to be recorded by the group, *Don't Pass Me By*, and George's songs were less Indian-influenced than had been expected. In fact, the only track that seemed less than straightforward was John's eight-minute plus *Revolution 9*, which was somewhat in the vein of his experimental work with Yoko. However, non-musical matters were also occupying the minds of The Beatles, particularly John and Paul.

Jane Asher, during a TV chat show, announced that Paul had broken off their engagement in July, while the following month, one day before her sixth wedding anniversary, Cynthia Lennon sued for divorce on the grounds of adultery. This personal fragmentation was also reflected in the recording of the 'double white' album, as it became known, and a number of the tracks found John and Paul record-

George Harrison.

ing their contributions separately, while both Yoko and Linda Eastman helped out with backing vocals, and George's friend Eric Clapton added lead guitar to several tracks, notably *While My Guitar Gently Weeps*.

Things were beginning to fall apart, coinciding with the publication of the authorized biography of the group by Hunter Davies.

During October, life became difficult for John Lennon and Yoko – they were arrested on drugs charges while spending the night at a flat in London belonging to Ringo, and a week later, it was announced that Yoko was expecting John's child. Two weeks after that, Linda Eastman arrived in London to stay with Paul, and in early 1969 they were married. At the start of November, George's soundtrack for the 'Wonderwall' film became the first solo LP by a Beatle to be released, beating by a few days *Two Virgins*, the album recorded earlier in the year by John and Yoko during their night spent at John's house. *Two Virgins* was particularly controversial, as its sleeve photograph was a full frontal study of John and Yoko, with both completely naked. EMI refused to release the album with such a sleeve, and eventually it came out via Track Records, a newly formed label owned by the managers of The Who, although when it was

displayed in shops, most record dealers disguised the sleeve with carefully cut out brown paper bags which allowed only the heads of John and Yoko to be seen. Shortly before the album finally reached the shops, Yoko was admitted to Queen Charlotte Hospital in Hammersmith, West London, as it was felt she was in danger of a miscarriage. Even there, John and she recorded what would become half of their next joint LP, one track of which is titled *Baby's Heartbeat*, and was recorded by pressing a microphone to Yoko's abdo-

Right: November 8, 1968. Cynthia Lennon at the Law Courts starting divorce proceedings against John.

Left: Paul, Ringo, a cartoon John Lennon and the genuine George in a publicity photograph for the 'Yellow Submarine' movie.

men. Whether or not this type of activity contributed to Yoko's eventual miscarriage will never be known, but on November 21, she lost the child she was expecting, and a week later, John was fined £150 on the drug charges, which he admitted, asking the court to pardon Yoko. George told the staff at Apple that he had invited some American friends, several of them Hell's Angels, to London, and wanted them to be looked after; and the cartoon feature, 'Yellow Submarine', was premièred to mixed reviews, much like those accorded Ringo's part in 'Candy' which was also shown for the first time. John and Yoko appeared on stage at London's Royal Albert Hall together inside a large white bag; and Ringo was rumoured to have told the others that he was leaving The Beatles. It was a desperately hectic conclusion to a very strange year.

Left: Crowds at the première of 'Yellow Submarine' entertained by living replicas of the cartoon characters in the film.

Yoko, Linda and The Split (1969-1970)

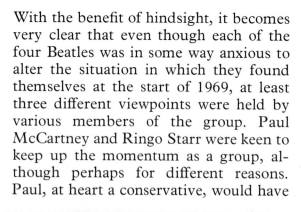

With the benefit of hindsight, it becomes very clear that even though each of the four Beatles was in some way anxious to alter the situation in which they found themselves at the start of 1969, at least three different viewpoints were held by various members of the group. Paul McCartney and Ringo Starr were keen to keep up the momentum as a group, although perhaps for different reasons. Paul, at heart a conservative, would have

John Lennon and Yoko Ono on the set of 'The Rolling Stones' Rock & Roll Circus'.

preferred that the status quo be maintained, no doubt hoping that he could resume what was undoubtedly a world-beating songwriting partnership with John, provided the latter could get over what was seen as simply an infatuation with Yoko. Ringo, a fledgling songwriter at best, saw little chance of even approaching the fame and wealth he had amassed as a Beatle without the others in front of him, despite his acting debut in 'Candy', and as the 1970s unfolded, it would become clear that such a pessimistic outlook was eventually justified. George Harrison was quite probably ambivalent about the future – having discovered in all things Indian, particularly Indian music, a new direction for his life, he no doubt realized that it was unlikely that the general public would share his enthusiasm for what he saw as the products of a higher spiritual plane, and was happy for The Beatles to continue recording as a group as long as he could also make his own records without the rest of them interfering. Which left John Lennon, who saw a new life opening before his eyes with promises of far greater fulfillment with Yoko Ono, in whom he saw the elusive qualities of a soul mate, something he had sought in vain in Cynthia, who was far more worldly and down to earth than her Japanese replacement.

By the end of the year it would be abundantly clear that things could never be quite the same again, but in early January the group assembled at Twickenham Film Studio to begin work on a new project, a documentary film that would show them recording a new album. For once, George Martin found himself not in sole control of the recording process, as another British engineer/producer, Glyn Johns, was invited by Paul McCartney to

be present as well. Johns had worked with the vast majority of the other First Division British groups of the 1960s, including The Rolling Stones, The Who and The Kinks, and had made a substantial impression with his production work on the first two LPs by American phenomenon Steve Miller during 1968. George Martin later recalled that the sessions were problematic from the start. The original intention had been to undertake both filming and recording at the newly opened Apple Studio. However, much of the equipment designed by Magic Alex had either not arrived or was unsuitable. Abbey Road was already booked, and earlier notions of performing a live concert proved impracticable for various reasons. It was necessary therefore to hire equipment from EMI and somehow fit it into the available space at Twickenham, which was made more difficult due to the

John and Yoko with John's son Julian in 1969, again during the filming of the circus movie featuring the Rolling Stones, which has never been publicly screened.

91

presence of the film crew. Both Johns and Martin independently maintain that the major aim of the group, but particularly John Lennon, was to revert to what was termed honesty, as opposed to the undoubtedly more listenable, but perhaps more contrived sound of their albums from *Revolver* onwards. The idea was praiseworthy, but its execution, due to the personal and business problems of the group, was more difficult to achieve. Nevertheless, early January saw numerous new tracks recorded. About this time, too, the possibility of another tour was mooted, but this was turned down point blank by George Harrison. The soundtrack album for the 'Yellow Submarine' film was also released during this period, although it was not the massive seller expected, largely due to the fact that only four new Beatle songs were included, and half the LP was taken up with George Martin's orchestral score of the film – four new songs, potential buyers obviously concluded, were insufficient for the price of a complete album.

However, the end of January saw something much more exciting, when the group, along with black keyboard player Billy Preston, decided to stage an informal concert in public on the roof of the Apple building in Savile Row, which would not only form part of the film, but, it was hoped, would also provide a new single. The plan was a substantial success, although nearby office workers were split in their reaction between those who were excited about the fact that The Beatles were playing together again, and others who were more concerned with their inability to concentrate due to the loud electric music ringing out from Apple. They could not be expected to appreciate that this would be the very last time The Beatles would play together before an audience. The outstanding track of the four songs that comprised the final performance by The Beatles was *Get Back*, written by Paul, who also takes lead vocal, and the Apple rooftop performance was one of the highlights of the film when it eventually emerged, although another version of the song, recorded in Apple Studios, was released as a single in April 1969. Not surprisingly, since it was a straightforward rock'n'roll song as opposed to some of the more fanciful items released by the group, it soared to the top of the charts in Britain and the rest of Europe, North America, Australasia and the Far East, and for many was a pleasant reaffirmation of The Beatles' ability to make great records. Behind the scenes, there were very different events occurring. Clive Epstein, who had been running NEMS since his brother's death,

Filming 'Let It Be' on the roof of the Apple building, from which the classic Get Back *resulted.*

entered into negotiations to sell the company. John Lennon had been quoted as saying in an interview that if the group were unable to stop losing money, he for one would have none left, which was the result of the over-generosity and lack of control with which Apple meandered from one day to the next, plus the incredible amount of pilfering that occurred due to the almost non-existent security.

NEMS was short of funds for a different reason – Brian Epstein's death had left the rest of his family, who were also the major shareholders in the company, with insufficient liquid assets to pay his substantial death duties, and the only easily saleable asset appeared to be NEMS itself, in which the group were themselves both minor shareholders and the biggest asset. An obvious move would have been for The Beatles to purchase NEMS, but they simply couldn't afford it due to the cost of running Apple. By the start of 1969, it had become clear to each of the group that they urgently needed some sort of financial adviser. An obvious candidate was the New York law firm of Eastman and Eastman, Lee Eastman being Linda's father and John Eastman her brother. They had greatly impressed Paul when he had met them, and it was becoming clear that unless anything changed drastically, he was likely to marry into the family. When the Eastmans heard that NEMS might be for sale, they got agreement from The Beatles to approach EMI for an advance against future royalties that could be used to acquire NEMS – curiously enough, the group had never received an advance of this type before, and it seemed a workable scheme.

Meanwhile, another New Yorker, an accountant named Allen Klein, read of John Lennon's shortage of funds, and decided to offer his services to sort out the group's finances. Klein had represented the Rolling Stones with great success for several years and acquired substantial amounts of money for them, which they were owed but which had been overlooked. Since Mick Jagger had spoken of Klein in glowing terms to Lennon, the latter was very happy to meet Klein to discuss ways of possibly rectifying the deteriorating situation. Precisely why John found him so very impressive that he was immediately ready to allow Klein to represent him is difficult to explain, al-

though apart from Jagger's recommendation and John's vague suspicion that Paul was perhaps trying to gain overall control of the group, Klein had also been effectively brought up by an aunt after his mother had died, which John conceivably saw as something both he and Klein had in common.

Clive Epstein had already been notified that The Beatles were interested in acquiring NEMS, and feeling an obligation to allow them to match any offer if they could, delayed the sale to an investment company that was under way. However, by that time The Beatles were split into

Peter Sellers (centre, with glasses) and Ringo (on Sellers' left) at a party thrown to mark the end of filming 'The Magic Christian'.

Right: A still from 'The Magic Christian' with Ringo dressed very formally in comparison with the rest of the cast.

several different camps, with Paul supporting the Eastmans, John opting for Klein, and George and Ringo somewhere in between but inclining towards Klein for largely the same reasons as John. The Eastmans were quick to inform Paul of Klein's reputation as an over-eager businessman, heavily involved in a good deal of litigation, but the other three members of the group were unconcerned by this, particularly when, at a meeting when all concerned were present, Klein provoked Lee Eastman into a verbal attack on him which aroused their sympathy for the man they saw as the innocent victim of Eastman's and Paul's ambitions. For a while, both Klein and the Eastmans could claim to represent The Beatles, the former as business manager and the latter as legal advisors. It was Klein's contention that it would be unnecessary to use the advance from EMI to purchase NEMS, as he believed he could prove that NEMS owed the group so much in payments of past royalties due to them that they would virtually hand over the company without any money being spent at all. Unfortunately, all the arguments delayed matters so much that the investment company that had originally begun nego-

tiations to buy NEMS were allowed, by default, to have it, whereupon the group told the new owners that NEMS would no longer represent them as agents.

Amid all this confusion, The Beatles had reportedly recorded around 100 songs during the sessions at Twickenham Studio and later at Apple, while 28 hours of film of them doing it were 'in the can'. A large percentage of the tracks have never seen the light of day legally, but the fact that there were so many recorded seems an obvious reason for this period of the group's career being the one most often represented on illegal bootleg records. Ringo, having completed work in the studios, began a second film, in fact another Terry Southern satire titled 'The Magic Christian', in which he had a far more major role as the adopted son of an eccentric millionaire played by Peter Sellers, the only star who was listed above Ringo in the credits, although there was a strong supporting cast including such household names as Christopher Lee, Yul Brynner, Spike Milligan and Raquel Welch. The movie was rather better received than 'Candy', and the sound-track included several songs by Apple signings Badfinger.

Soon after Ringo began filming, Paul and Linda confirmed the speculation that had existed for some time by getting married on March 12, 1969, coincidentally the same day that police raided George's home in Esher, and found a quantity of marijuana. Eight days later, on March 20, John and Yoko (whose divorce from her second husband had been finalized a few weeks before), went to Paris for a holiday and spent half a day in Gibraltar, where they were married with Peter Brown from Apple as best man. After that, they flew to Amsterdam to spend a week's honeymoon in bed, as a demonstration for world peace. Almost inevitably, they also embarked on some recording during their 'Bed-In', as it was called, and the results, which were of no greater interest than their previous recordings, were later released as *The Wedding Album*. During April, John and Yoko worked on another recording, but since Paul was also present, the results were much more constructive. This was *The Ballad Of John And Yoko*, a somewhat autobiographical song relating the prob-

Left: George and Patti Harrison arriving at Esher and Walton Magistrates' Court to face drugs charges during 1969.

Below: Paul McCartney and Linda on the way to their wedding with Linda's six-year-old daughter Heather.

Above: John and Yoko wearing a 'bag of peace' on BBC-TV's 'Today' show.

lems the two had faced in recent months, and was released while *Get Back* was still high in the charts. Despite it being a comparatively ordinary single, it topped the British charts, although in America, it peaked only just inside the Top Ten, largely as a result of being banned from radio play in some areas due to a portion of the chorus, in which John sings 'Christ you know it ain't easy, You know how hard it can be, The way things are going, They're going to crucify me'. On the same day that the track was recorded, John changed his middle name by deed poll from Winston to Ono, but more serious matters would unfold two weeks later. In early May 1969, John, George and Ringo formally appointed Allen Klein as their manager, outvoting Paul, who did not add his signature to the legal document. Klein immediately moved his operation into the Apple building, and embarked on a swift, but thorough, campaign of firing virtually the entire staff of the company, including several employees who had been working for The Beatles for many years, like Peter Asher and Alistair Taylor, who had been Brian Epstein's personal assistant and was a personal friend of each of The Beatles. The only executives to avoid being dismissed were Peter Brown and Neil Aspinall, although Klein apparently did his utmost to dispose of them like all the others, but was unable to convince the

Right: John and Yoko pictured during the press conference to launch their 'Bed In for peace' at the Hilton Hotel, Amsterdam.

group that their longtime allies should be fired.

The day after Klein's appointment, two more Beatle albums were released, bringing both John and George's total of solo recordings to two LPs each. John and Yoko's *Life With The Lions* differed little from *Two Virgins*, except insofar as one side was recorded at a concert in Cambridge a few months before, and briefly featured two other musicians in addition to Yoko's free form 'vocals' and John's feedback experiments on guitar. The other side of the record consisted of the recordings made during Yoko's miscarriage, and also includes a self-explanatory track entitled *Two Minutes Silence*. It was not a massive seller, and neither was George's *Electronic Sound*, on which can be heard Harrison's early experiments with a newly acquired synthesizer. These new releases briefly deflected attention from another business crisis that had been taking place over the previous months. Dick James, who had been the publisher of The Beatles' music from early in their career (and had become very rich as a result) had decided to sell his share of their publishing company, Northern Songs, to ATV Music. Although the group themselves actually owned only a minor part of the company, they felt that their personal property was being sold without their consent, and endeavoured to raise sufficient finance to buy James' share. In the event, they were nearly successful, but it has been suggested that the company's other shareholders, who were able to outvote The Beatles, were concerned at the possibility of Allen Klein having an executive position in Northern Songs, and preferred Sir Lew Grade, a man with a lengthy track record of success in commercial terms.

At this point, the Lennons, with Yoko's child from a former marriage, Kyoko, decided to take their message of peace further afield. Where better than as close to the United States as possible, like Canada? On May 26, 1969, they checked into the Queen Elizabeth Hotel in Montreal after being reportedly held up for over two hours before immigration officials would allow them into the country, and began another 'Bed In for Peace', which lasted ten days. During this period, they were visited by a number of well-known admirers, including Timothy

Leary, the one-time scientist who had publicized the drug LSD in glowing terms, disc jockey Murray The K, who had been a great source of support to The Beatles during their first visits to America, beat poet Allen Ginsberg, black American comedian Dick Gregory, and one of the Smothers Brothers. Many of this crew were present at the start of June when John and Yoko decided to record a song they had written together, *Give Peace A Chance*, which was subsequently released credited to The Plastic Ono Band. John naturally wanted his latest masterpiece generally available as soon as possible, and

Above: John and Yoko meeting Yoko's daughter, Kyoko Cox, on her arrival in London from New York.

Right: John and Yoko on television during their peace campaign with TV personality Eamonn Andrews.

release was set for July 4 (no doubt a symbolic date), with a lunch to be held at Chelsea Town Hall the day before, at which John and Yoko would explain their message of peace to the world. Unfortunately, two days earlier, the car in which they were travelling around Scotland on a brief holiday was involved in a serious accident that hospitalized John, Yoko and Kyoko, who were thus unable to attend the party, but sent Ringo instead, who was amiable enough without seeming to feel quite as committed to the project as the Lennons evidently were. Paul wasn't there, because he was back at Abbey Road working with George Martin on a new Beatles LP. Martin later recalled that he was somewhat surprised to hear from Paul, after the fiasco over the previous album (which had still not emerged at this point), and was guarded in his answers to McCartney's request for him to produce the group again, indicating that he would be very happy to produce the group, as long as they agreed to be produced, and would follow his instructions. Martin was surprised when Paul agreed to these and other conditions, and a number of tracks recorded during the abortive sessions earlier in the year were completed or re-worked, although each of The Beatles

preferred working on their own compositions, and had to be cajoled into helping out on songs written by others. In the circumstances, the resulting LP, *Abbey Road*, contains more excellent tracks than might have been expected, including *Come Together* by John, *Something* and *Here Comes The Sun* by George and several creditable compositions by Paul. It was a great success around the world, record buyers expressing an almost audible sigh or relief that the group appeared to have put their differences and their solo projects aside. Unfortunately, it was also to be last time that The Beatles would work together as a group.

Give Peace A Chance had been a sizeable hit, although not as big as *The Ballad Of John And Yoko*, and John Lennon was determined to pursue this aspect of his career under the name of the Plastic Ono Band. During the 'Bed In' in Toronto, some visitors had indicated that they intended to stage a Peace Festival in Toronto later in the year, and had asked whether John and Yoko might participate. It would appear that John gave no definite answer at the time, but when the organizers had telephoned him at Apple during early September, indicating that plans had gone ahead and the concert was

to be held a few days later, John impulsively decided that he must be there. A private jet was organized, and a pick-up band recruited of Eric Clapton on guitar, Klaus Voorman, an old friend from Hamburg who had by this time settled in Britain and played with several well known acts, on bass, plus drummer Alan White. This group, who had never played together before, were to be the latest version of the Plastic Ono Band, and rehearsed a set of eight songs on the plane crossing the Atlantic, and on September 13, 1969, were surprise guest stars at a concert whose bill also included rock'n'roll legends like Chuck Berry, Bo Diddley, Little Richard and Gene Vincent. Half the set, which lasted for less than forty minutes, consisted of rock'n'roll oldies and Lennon originals, one of which, *Cold Turkey*, would become the next Plastic Ono Band single, while the other half was dominated by Yoko, who wrote the two songs concerned. The concert, if not necessarily the performance, was a great success, and marked John's return to playing in front of an audience for the first time since 1966.

At the end of October, a studio recording of *Cold Turkey* by the Plastic Ono Band (with Ringo replacing Alan White)

was released, and its bleak sound was obviously of less interest to record buyers than a single coupling *Something* and *Come Together* from the *Abbey Road* album, which was a big hit. In fact, it had been Allen Klein's idea to release the single by The Beatles in Britain, after it had accelerated up the American charts, but a by product which no one obviously foresaw was that it might divert attention from *Cold Turkey*, which is what seems to have happened. John Lennon, in typically frivolous manner, (and probably irked that *The Wedding Album*, his latest experimental album with Yoko, was being ignored, despite its extremely opulent packaging in a box which, apart from the record, contained such useful items as a photograph of a piece of wedding cake and a copy of his marriage certificate) returned his M.B.E. to the Queen on November 25 with a note that said he was protesting about Britain's involvement in a war in West Africa and support of the United States in Vietnam, and because *Cold Turkey* was slipping down the charts. Two weeks later, the flood of Lennon material continued with the release of recordings made at the Toronto Peace Festival titled *Live Peace In Toronto*, but

100

this was as unsuccessful as *The Wedding Album* in penetrating the British charts, and seemed to indicate that in Britain at least, the public were beginning to tire of John's curious output.

George Harrison, meanwhile, had been experiencing a good deal of success with musical projects unconnected with The Beatles. His friendship with Eric Clapton had blossomed, and a song the two had written together, *Badge*, was a big hit, with George being credited for his part as a performer on the record as 'L'Angelo Mysterioso'. He had also been busy producing other acts signed to Apple Records, and had met with some chart action with the Radha Krishna Temple, a group of disciples of Indian religions who chanted the *Hare Krishna Mantra* and with Billy Preston, the keyboard player who had guested on *Get Back* and who scored a world-wide hit with *That's The Way God Planned It*, both of which George produced. He also worked with less success with other Apple signings like Jackie Lomax, a friend from Liverpool who had been in a Merseybeat group called The Undertakers, and Doris Troy, a black American soul singer. Paul spent much of the autumn with Linda on a farm

they had purchased in Scotland, and it was at this point that alarming rumours began to circulate that he had died. This preposterous story was apparently started by an American college student, and finally reached the ears of a radio station executive in Detroit who broadcast it as fact, supporting the story with a number of 'clues' which, it was said, indicated that Paul had been killed in a car accident during November 1966. A researcher confirmed that a violent accident had occurred on the given day, and that one of the passengers, a dark haired male, was so badly disfigured that he was unrecognizable, his head having been severed from his body. The other three Beatles were then supposed to have held a 'Paul lookalike' contest, the winner of which was a young man from Scotland named William Campbell, who was employed to become Paul, although to allow the subterfuge to remain undetected, no winner of the contest was ever announced publicly. Subsequently, Beatle records and sleeves had included 'clues', in order that Paul's fans should realize the 'truth' in as gentle a manner as possible. Of the four aural 'clues', only two are distinguishable as sounding remotely like what is claimed for

Above: George with members of the Society of Krishna Conciousness, on the day 'Hare Krishna' mantra was released as a single (above).

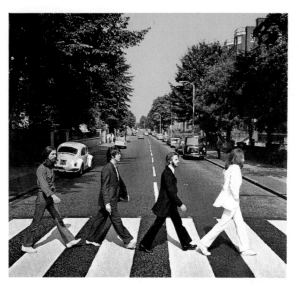

Right: Sleeve to Abbey Road, *the final LP recorded by The Beatles, which was released in September, 1969.*

Opposite: One of the last press handout pictures of The Beatles, a photo session which also produced the sleeve picture for the Hey Jude *LP when it was released nearly ten years later in Britain.*

them, while the line in *A Day In The Life* referring to someone 'blowing their mind out in a car' is fairly definitely not referring to Paul, but to John's friend, Tara Browne, and can be discounted as a 'clue' on every level. A little more convincing for would-be sleuths is a voice which appears at the very end of *Strawberry Fields Forever* and appears to say 'I buried Paul'.

It was somewhat easier to inspect the visual 'clues' on various record sleeves. The 'Sergeant Pepper' album sleeve collage supposedly portrays The Beatles (presumably with Mr. Campbell standing in for Paul) grouped around a grave, close to which is a bass guitar, and a flower arrangement which spells out (albeit roughly) the word 'Paul'. Above Paul's head is a raised hand, which is supposedly an Indian death sign, and another raised hand behind Paul also appeared on the *Yellow Submarine* sleeve. Reverting to *Sergeant Pepper*, the picture of The Beatles on the rear of the sleeve shows Paul with his back to the camera, although there is a definite explanation for this which makes the 'clue' worthless – when the photograph in question was taken, Paul was in America with Jane Asher, who was celebrating her 21st birthday while on tour with the Bristol Old Vic Repertory Company, and in order that the photo session, which was urgently required, should proceed, Mal Evans was recruited to wear the clothes worn elsewhere on the sleeve by Paul, but of necessity had to stand with his back to the camera. On the centre spread photograph, Paul is wearing a badge with the letters 'O.P.D.' on it, which was said to be an abbreviation for 'Officially Pronounced Dead', but in fact

was something he picked up while in Canada – it is actually short for 'Ontario Police Department', and was given to Paul by a friendly police officer. The *Magical Mystery Tour* sleeve was similarly bedecked with 'clues', especially since it contained a 24 page booklet. Two more instances of Paul with a hand raised behind his head, a picture of Paul sitting at a desk upon which is a sign containing the words 'I Was', and another picture of Paul in which he is not wearing shoes – a custom in certain parts of the world was to bury dead people whose feet would be bare. But the clue which seemed the most relevant one came from a picture of the four Beatles wearing white suits and with carnations in their button holes – each of the other three has a red carnation, but Paul's is black!

All the above information was noticed retrospectively following the release of *Abbey Road*, which seems to have been the album which sparked off the controversy. The front sleeve photograph shows the group walking across Abbey Road in single file, and over-ripe flights of fancy interpreted this as a funeral procession, with John as the officiating clergyman, George (in working clothes, apparently) as the grave digger, Paul (with bare feet again!) as the deceased and Ringo as a mourner. A car parked nearby has a number plate of '281F', which was taken to mean that Paul would have been 28 if he had lived, although in fact he was only 27 in 1969, when the photograph was taken. However, some Eastern religions (in which The Beatles were interested at the time) maintain that each new born child is already a year old when it emerges into the world, which validates the 'clue' . . . Reverting to the 'funeral procession', Paul is out of step with the others, and the word 'Beatles' on the sleeve has a crack in it, both items indicating that the group was in some way incomplete . . .

While the uncovering of his 'death' was causing headlines throughout America – in Britain, the stories were correctly dismissed as the work of sensationalists – Paul was in Scotland wondering about his group's next move. His suggestions of playing live again, even if in some unannounced capacity, had been rejected by John who apparently found the experience of playing with the Plastic Ono Band so invigorating that he announced a

decided preference for working without the rest of The Beatles in future. Paul had become a father during the summer, when Linda had given birth to their first child, who was named Mary after Paul's late mother, and when life had returned to normal, was anxious to make some music, if only for his own benefit. He thus began to record virtually as a one man band, playing bass, guitar and drums, which he carefully overdubbed until he had completed a backing track, after which he added his own vocals. Some of the recording was done at Abbey Road, more at another North London studio, and the balance at his house in St John's Wood. Ringo also started to record a solo album, using songs which his mother liked from the past, such as *Have I Told You Lately That I Love You* and *You Always Hurt The One You Love*. George Martin agreed to produce Ringo's LP, and an interesting scheme was instituted whereby a number of different arrangers were used, each providing an instrumental backing track without vocals, which George Martin would supervise with Ringo. When the album, *Sentimental Journey*, appeared the following year, it was not an enormous success, since the choice of material (much of which was well known in versions by notable singers of the 1940s and 1950s) was some way from rock'n'roll, added to which Ringo's slightly colourless voice did not compare favourably with,

Above: John and Yoko protest about the death of convicted criminal James Hanratty during 1969.

Right: John and Yoko meet the parents of Hanratty, executed after being found guilty of murder, and (right) the writer of a pamphlet protesting the dead man's innocence.

for example, Doris Day, the Ink Spots or Les Paul and Mary Ford, who had recorded classic versions of the songs.

George was also busy at the end of 1969, although not in the recording studio. He too was once again appearing on stages all over Britain, as a low profile guest among the musicians backing Delaney and Bonnie Bramlett, a husband and wife team who were at one point to have their LP, *Accept No Substitute*, released on Apple, but somehow at the last minute signed with another label. The Bramletts were very friendly with Eric Clapton, whose shortlived band, Blind Faith, had worked with them in America, and when Clapton agreed to tour with Delaney and Bonnie in Britain, he brought along his friend, George. Although it would not become widely known until some years later, Eric Clapton had begun to fall in love with George's wife, Patti.

At the end of 1969, John and Yoko performed at a benefit concert for the United Nation Children's Fund, UNICEF, at London's Lyceum Ballroom, and both George and Eric, along with other members of Delaney and Bonnie's band, formed what was called the Plastic Ono Supergroup when live recordings of the concert were released three years later. Paul was not involved with the concert, and perhaps more surprisingly, neither was Ringo. The following day saw John and Yoko's return to Canada on another stage of their 'peace mission', and among those with whom they met during their week in the country were rock'n'roll star Ronnie Hawkins, journalist Marshall McLuhan who interviewed them for Canadian television, and members of the Canadian Government, including Premier Pierre Trudeau, with whom they discussed plans for a projected

Above: John and Yoko (both in white) on stage at London's Lyceum Ballroom for the UNICEF Peace Concert in 1969. Among the other musicians are Eric Clapton (on Yoko's right) playing guitar and wearing overcoat and Delaney & Bonnie Bramlett (between Yoko and Eric).

Peace Festival to take place in Toronto during the following summer. After Christmas, the Lennons moved on to Denmark to see Kyoko, who was staying with her father, Anthony Cox, Yoko's second ex-husband. At the end of a hectic year for each of The Beatles, although especially so for John Lennon, the future of the group remained uncertain.

1970 was not only the beginning of a new decade, but also the start of a new era for The Beatles, during which most of their work would emerge in solo form, although perhaps rather less impressively

Below: John and Yoko leaving London for Toronto on another peace mission in December 1969.

than either they or their many fans would have preferred. Inevitably, it was John and Yoko who first made the headlines during the year, having their hair cut extremely short as another symbol in their quest for peace. Yoko had been releasing records under her own name during the previous year, either as collaborations with John like *Two Virgins* and the other Lennon albums, or as B sides to John's singles, like *Remember Love*, which she sang and was released as the B side of *Give Peace A Chance*, and for the third Plastic Ono Band single (and the first of 1971), she as usual contributed the B side, *Who Has Seen The Wind*. John's side of the single, *Instant Karma*, was produced by Phil Spector, the remarkable American who had created a number of unforgettable classics during the 1960s for acts like The Crystals, The Ronettes, Ike and Tina Turner and the Righteous Brothers. Latterly, Spector was presumed to have retired from production on any more than an occasional basis, his lack of production work being apparently explained by the comparative failure of one of his finest records, *River Deep – Mountain High* by Ike and Tina Turner, which was a big hit in Britain, but which flopped in America. Thus, in early 1970, Spector was regarded as having passed his peak, and it must have come as a pleasant surprise when he was invited by Allen Klein to 'salvage' the recordings made for the film documentary, which remained unreleased although they were at least a year old. However, before Spector was allowed to try to construct something meaningful out of the dozens of boxes of tape, it was insisted that he prove he was still capable of inspired production work by producing a single, the most appropriate vehicle being the one John Lennon was about to record, When *Instant Karma* was released during February 1970, it sounded quite unlike many of Spector's previous productions – his celebrated 'Wall of Sound', created by, for example, recording several guitarists playing the same passage in unison, seemed to be absent, and a more sparse approach had been used. However, the single was successful enough (Top Ten on both sides of the Atlantic) for Spector to receive the green light for the much bigger project of sorting out the mess of tapes recorded by The Beatles with Glyn Johns (and in part with George Martin). Even so, it was Martin who was credited with producing what would be the final single released in Britain by The Beatles before the eventual split became public knowledge, and the song selected, *Let It Be*, was also used as the title of the documentary film, which was being prepared for public consumption at the same time.

Although this was far from a happy period for the group, *Let It Be* remains one of the group's finest performances – Paul's lead vocal and piano seem retrospectively in complete contrast to the furore that was part of each of The Beatles' daily lives, with Allen Klein (still not supported by McCartney) taking decisions on the group's behalf that he could not be sure, due to his frosty relationship with Paul, would eventually be acted upon. Three weeks later, Ringo's *Sentimental Journey* album was released to a bemused reaction – although it had been made clear that the LP was intended for the drummer's mother and his other relatives primarily, Beatle fans seemingly expected something other than what was delivered, but when Paul McCartney's first solo record, an album simply titled

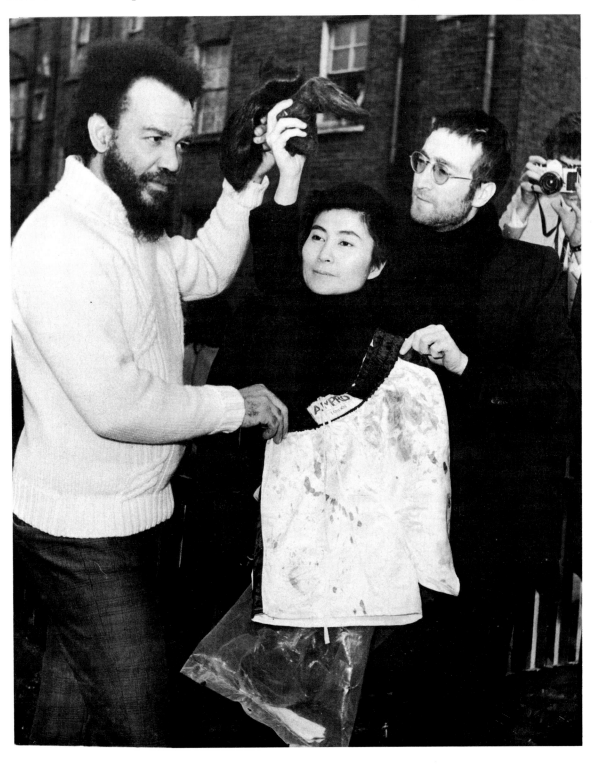

Left: John and Yoko give black power leader Michael X clumps of their recently shorn hair, while in return they receive a pair of shorts said to have been worn by the then Cassius Clay (now known as Muhammad Ali). As usual, the bizarre exchange was said to be in the interests of peace.

Right: More peace propaganda on BBC-TV's 'Top Of The Pops', with Plastic Ono Band drummer Alan White on the right.

McCartney, reached the shops three weeks later, the consternation was still greater. Paul had played every instrumental part of the album himself as well as doing nearly all the vocals, with Linda contributing a few background vocal parts, but more to the point, the songs, lacking the input of the other Beatles (and particularly the harder-edged sensibility that John Lennon provided) seemed for the most part weak and sentimental, in the same way that John's own solo work with the Plastic Ono Band appeared unnecessarily brittle. There was a general feeling of dissatisfaction among purchasers of the album, many of whom no doubt acquired it without first hearing it, as they would for a normal Beatles LP, since it had registered advance sales of over two million copies in America. The sole exception was *Maybe I'm Amazed*, which later became a highlight of the repertoire of The Faces, for whom Rod Stewart, at the time still somewhat of an unknown quantity, was vocalist.

Paul's insistence that his album be released in April 1969 caused some argument among The Beatles, as by this time Phil Spector had completed work on the recordings made during the film project, which were to be released as the *Let It Be* album. Obviously, *Let It Be* and *McCartney*, if released almost simultaneously,

would result in neither album receiving its just commercial deserts, as sales would be split, and eventually Paul was allowed to have his way and *Let It Be* was delayed until the first part of May, with the première of the film held two weeks later. *Let It Be* was packaged in a box with a full-colour paperback book titled 'The Beatles Get Back', incorporating stills and apparently unused dialogue from the film, although six months later, the box and the book were no longer supplied and the record was made available in standard form. Despite the higher than normal price for a single album (to cover the cost of the book), *Let It Be* sold prodigiously, with advance orders of nearly four million copies (at a gross retail value of over $25,000,000) in the United States, where it topped the charts as it did in Britain. However, the LP is not regarded as one of the Beatles' finest, due in part to the problems that surrounded the original recording of the tracks, and perhaps also because Phil Spector's production was at times seen as inappropriate – Paul McCartney is said to have disapproved strongly of the manner in which Spector added an orchestral backing to his song *The Long And Winding Road*, even though, in Spector's defence, the track was released as a single in America and topped the charts a few weeks after the single version of *Let It Be* had vacated the Number One position.

As for the film, a measure of how interested and committed each of The Beatles felt on the subject was that none of them were present at the première, while critics were quick to note that virtually no one but the group themselves appeared on the screen, which made it seem rather contrived, and the movie was relatively quickly forgotten, although since the soundtrack music had not been reworked by Phil Spector, it was perhaps closer to the original intention of 'honest'. By this time, the public had been informed via the newspapers that Paul McCartney, in a press handout accompanying his solo LP, had stated that he felt that the Lennon-McCartney songwriting partnership was over, and that, at least temporarily, he no longer considered himself to be a member of The Beatles. While John had been cajoled into suppressing an identical statement the previous autumn by Allen Klein,

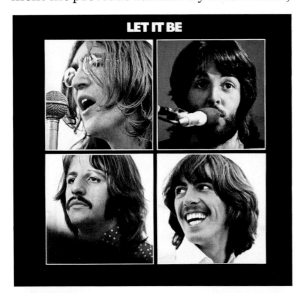

Paul was not inclined to do anything to prolong an arrangement he felt had gone on too long, and the final straw probably came when he appealed to Klein to restore *The Long And Winding Road* to its original condition, and was told that no changes would be made. There would be no new releases by The Beatles for nearly three years, although a feeling existed that everything would return to normal after the group had spent some time apart.

John Lennon and Yoko Ono continued to spend their time investigating methods of promoting world peace, although they withdrew their support from the projected Peace Festival to be held in Canada after discovering that the proceeds were intended for profit rather than peace. In April 1970, they visited the clinic of an American psychiatrist named Dr. Arthur Janov, who had written a book, 'The Primal Scream', which propounded his theories about how many of the problems and insecurities felt by everyone were the result of a childhood during which love and basic security were sometimes missing. So impressed were the Lennons by Janov's theories – they had begun to bicker incessantly, according to the few people who ever saw them – that they decided to telephone Janov and ask to be enrolled in his clinic as patients. The doctor agreed to visit them at their home in Ascot, where he began a course of treatment during which both confessed their childhood fears and anxieties, and apparently screamed and cried – according to Janov, letting all their repressed emotions out into the open would help them to discover their real selves. After that, they returned with Janov to his clinic in Los Angeles to continue the 'treatment' over a period of several months, before returning to Britain at the end of the summer, after which both began work on solo albums, although it would appear that while John featured on Yoko's tracks, she was less involved with his undertaking. Phil Spector was again engaged by John as producer, in many ways a rather thankless task since John's new songs were nearly all written during his period under the influence of Dr. Janov, and were mostly very bleak lyrically. With a minimal backing provided by Klaus Voorman on bass and the faithful Ringo on drums, the album has not become any easier to enjoy over the years. The same rhythm

Left: Sleeve to the last original Beatles LP released during the group's lifetime.

Left: The somewhat anonymous sleeve to McCartney, *Paul's first solo LP.*

section was used for Yoko's LP, her first actual solo album as all her previous releases had been in company with John, and both albums had a similar photograph on the front of the sleeve, with Yoko resting on John's lap on her album, and the positions reversed for his. The records were simultaneously released two weeks before Christmas 1970, and for once, those who felt that Yoko's records were substantially less intersting than John's could be pardoned for doubting that the assertion was still true, although the on-going acceptance in America of anything connected with The Beatles, irrespective of quality – even Ringo's solo album sold more than half a million copies – resulted in John's album selling a million copies within six weeks of release, while even Yoko's made a brief showing near the foot

of the chart. However, a single released in America with one of John's tracks, *Mother*, coupled with one of Yoko's *Why*, failed to reach the Top 40.

Two other Beatle (or ex-Beatle) albums were released before John and Yoko's 'companion' albums during 1970. Ringo, not discouraged by the slightly bewildered reception accorded his first solo effort (although some suggest that he was anxious to atone for the somewhat uninspired nature of *Sentimental Journey*) had met Pete Drake, a pedal steel guitar player from Nashville, while both were working on a new album by George Harrison, and when Ringo mentioned that he was interested in making a country & western album, Drake was pleased to offer his services as producer and organizer, provided that Ringo would make the record in Nashville, which he said would only take two days. Ringo agreed, and spent the requisite time in the studio on the last day of June and the first day of July, emerging with an adequate, if less than overwhelming LP of straightforward country music titled *Beaucoups Of Blues*, which was released during September 1970. Somewhat surprisingly, in view of its obvious superiority to *Sentimental Journey*, the album was less successful in chart terms than its predecessor, although the title track was released as a single in America and became a minor hit.

While Ringo's attempts to establish some kind of career for himself as a singer were never likely to be met with immediate success, and he was conceivably more concerned about the impending birth of his and Maureen's third child, Lee, George Harrison had been quietly making progress with his first straightforward (as opposed to Indian and/or experimental) solo album. Pete Drake was flown in from Nashville to add pedal steel parts to some of the songs, having been recommended by no less a person than Bob Dylan, who was himself represented on the album as a songwriter, contributing *I'd Have You Anytime*, which he and George had co-written in 1968, and *If Not For You*. George himself had amassed a sizeable number of songs over the years, some of those included on *All Things Must Pass*, (as the album was titled) being up to four years old. Perhaps in view of the fact that he had so much material at his disposal, George and a varying crew of supporting musicians, of whom only Ringo was also a Beatle, recorded 23 tracks, and decided to release them as a triple album in a box, although the third record was slightly different from its fellows, as each of the four main songs was the result of studio jam sessions, and the LP itself was subtitled *Apple Jam*. Several more significant features of the album would make a deep impression on George in years to come, the first concerning his great friend, Eric Clapton, who inevitably became involved when George began recording.

Aside from his growing infatuation for Patti Harrison, Clapton was searching for a new musical direction for himself, after having been involved with two so-called 'supergroups', Cream and Blind Faith. Following the dissolution of Blind Faith,

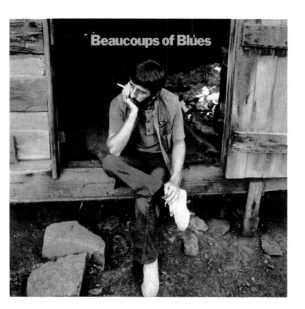

Left: Sleeve to Ringo's 1970 solo LP, Beaucoups Of Blues.

Below: A scene at the mixing desk during 'Let It Be', with Yoko and John inseparable and the other three Beatles seemingly taking a less active part in the proceedings.

Above: A contented Ringo posing with a metal apple during the early 1970s.

Clapton invited two of the players, drummer Jim Gordon and bass player Carl Radle, to join him in a new group, which was completed by another Delaney and Bonnie associate, keyboard player Bobby Whitlock, and one of the new quartet's first tasks was to act as the backing band for George Harrison's recording sessions, which were produced, once again, by Phil Spector, who by this time was functioning as head of A&R for Apple Records. Clapton, having endured for some time the reputation as the finest blues guitarist in the world, which he felt he did not deserve, was anxious for the new band to be relatively anonymous, and chose the name of Derek and the Dominoes to indicate that he was purely a member, and not necessarily the leader, of the new group. As they were already in the studio working with George and Phil Spector, Clapton & Co. took the opportunity to cut some tracks with Spector producing, with a view to his producing their first album after George's record was completed, but obviously some kind of personality clash occurred, because only one track by Derek and the Dominoes produced by Spector has ever been officially released. Following the unsuccessful session with Spector, Clapton and his band eventually recorded their only studio album, the double LP *Layla*, with another producer, but the title track was in fact an impassioned love song addressed to Patti, who later left George and married Eric.

Before George realized that he would suffer a personal loss following on from the album, a more pressing problem arose as a result of the best-known song on *All Things Must Pass*, a devotional anthem written by George and titled *My Sweet Lord*, which topped the American charts for four weeks at the end of 1970, and the British charts for six weeks in early 1971. Everyone seemed to feel that it reminded them of a song that had been a big hit for an American all-girl group named the Chiffons in 1963, *He's So Fine*, but George firmly denied that he was plagiarizing another tune. Finally, the publishers of *He's So Fine* took legal action against him, and after a lengthy legal battle, an American court eventually found against George, who had to pay compensation of over half a million dollars to the publishers of *He's So Fine* in 1976.

he had toured with Delaney and Bonnie, inviting George along for the ride, but early in 1970, most of the musicians who had worked with the Bramletts were recruited by Leon Russell to form a large band to back Joe Cocker, who was under threat of a heavy fine if he failed to undertake a massive American tour to which he was contracted. The resulting trip around America was filmed and recorded under the title of *Mad Dogs And Englishmen*, but after two months of hard work, the unwieldy group disbanded, leaving a number of excellent players at a loose end.

Nevertheless, *All Things Must Pass* came as a very pleasant surprise to Beatle fans all over the world – while it was believed that George was a reasonable songwriter and above average singer, no one had really expected him to come up with what was certainly the most impressive solo album by a Beatle thus far. It became the first three LP set to top the British charts, which it did for seven weeks, a similar period to the time it spent at Number One in America. From nowhere, George was suddenly the most successful solo Beatle and the first of the four to top both singles and album charts on both sides of the Atlantic (although Paul's first solo album was the first record by an inidividual Beatle to reach Number One). While speaking of Paul, the end of 1970 saw the final nails being hammered into the coffin of The Beatles, as Paul issued a writ against the company he jointly owned with them, asking that their partnership be dissolved forthwith. John

Lennon, meanwhile, had asserted in an interview that the reason for the Beatles breaking up was that Paul had tried to become the leader of the group. It had been a terrible year for Beatles fans everywhere, and could have been a good deal pleasanter for the group themselves.

Left: The sleeve of George's first solo album, All Things Must Pass, *released in 1970.*

Below: George Harrison (right) with Ravi Shankar (third right) and the other Indian performers featured in the first Festival Of the Arts of India in September 1970.

The Solo Years (1971-1972)

The start of 1971 found each of The Beatles in a dilemma, although each of them had quite different problems. John was about to unceremoniously drop his infatuation with primal therapy for a new crusading interest, although whether the slightly bemused reception to his latest album was a contributory factor cannot be accurately judged – after all, it was a big seller. He and Yoko spent most of their time in one room (the main bedroom) of their mansion in Ascot, Tittenhurst Park. Yoko was seemingly feeling more and more upset over the fact that she was distanced from her daughter Kyoko, who was living with her father, Yoko's ex-husband Tony Cox, in America, and was anxious that the child should live with her – this situation would erupt later in the year. Also, although John was not aware of

Below: An estate-agent's eye view of Tittenhurst Park, Ascot, where John and Yoko lived before moving to the U.S.A.

it at the time, his peace promotions, which led to a number of dissident Americans crossing his path – he was perhaps too naïve to understand that in most cases, they simply wanted to use his fame to further their own, often rather dubious, causes – had been noted by American governmental security specialists, who apparently issued a confidential memorandum about his potentially subversive activities at the start of 1971.

Paul spent much of the early part of 1971 in New York, perhaps to be less accessible to the other Beatles following his move at the end of 1970 to wind up the group's affairs but also because he claimed that he was in search of a drummer whom he could use on future recording projects – he had done all the drumming on the *McCartney* LP himself, but while he was perfectly adequate on the kit, was less confident than on guitar, bass or piano, and felt the need for an expert who might also act as a sounding board, since Linda's lack of musical experience, as well as her personal relationship with Paul, led him to be unsure of the validity of her comments. Paul held auditions secretly, eventually choosing a relatively obscure session musician, Denny Seiwell, who had moved from his Pennsylvania birthplace to work with New York jazz groups before infiltrating the busy studio scene. Seiwell's first record with the McCartneys was a single, *Another Day*, which reached the Top Three of the British singles chart, and also made the U.S. Top Five. By the time it was released, Paul had started work on his second post-Beatles album, again using Seiwell, as well as two other American session musicians, Hugh McCracken and David Spinozza, who both played guitar, and even the New York Philharmonic Orchestra here and there. Inevitably, the additional musicians gave the LP a more polished feel than *McCartney*'s somewhat 'home made' impression.

George Harrison was still to some extent basking in the adulation accorded *All Things Must Pass* and *My Sweet Lord*, but on the domestic front, matters were less idyllic. In the wake of his infatuation with India and spiritual matters, he had abandoned drug taking and alcohol and become a vegetarian. He spent many hours each day meditating, and although his wife Patti (who had been responsible for first recommending the Maharishi)

Above: The McCartney family arriving at London Airport in 1971 after a trip to America.

Left: George Harrison pictured during the early 1970s.

A still from '200 Motels'
featuring Ringo as Frank
Zappa.

had tried to share George's interests, she was anxious to have children, and a family obviously didn't figure among George's priorities at that time. After the drug raid on their house in Esher, George had purchased a remarkable mansion near Henley on Thames, to the west of London – Friar Park, which stood in more than 30 acres of grounds, and had been allowed to deteriorate over the previous fifty years, following the death of the Victorian anti-clerical eccentric who had rebuilt the estate at the end of the nineteenth century, Sir Francis Crisp. Crisp had made his fortune working as a solicitor and his mental sharpness had also been utilized by prominent politicians, but much of his leisure was spent in creating a residence for himself which supposedly bears some resemblance to the Palace of Versailles. His disregard for contemporary religion was manifested in the mansion by the use of brass door knobs shaped like the heads of monks for every room, plus a statue in the grounds of a monk holding a frying pan riddled with holes, in front of which stood a plaque which read 'Two holy friars'. A succession of owners had lived at Friar Park until the early 1950s, when it had been bought for use as a convent (after the monks' head door handles had been removed) until around 1970, when it was

put on the market, but had attracted little interest and remained empty for a year until George saw it. He embarked on an extensive renovation programme supervised by his brothers, Harry and Peter, but this new interest, combined with his continuing support for Indian religious movements – he had produced two hits for the Radha Krishna Temple, a group of 'Hare Krishna' chanters, in 1969–70 – left him very little time for Patti, whom he obviously considered to be eternally faithful to him.

Ringo, as ever, was the Beatle without much to do, so that when he was invited by Frank Zappa, leader of the intellectually stimulating but commercially inaccessible Mothers of Invention to appear in a film Zappa was making, '200 Motels', he was pleased to take part, although he was probably as confused by the script as everyone else involved, among whom were Keith Moon, drummer with The Who, Jewish folksinger/actor Theodore Bikel and even Ringo's chauffeur Martin Lickert, who was prevailed upon to work as bass player with the Mothers. Ringo's role was non-musical – he played Larry the Dwarf, who appeared disguised as Frank Zappa in the film (while Zappa also appeared as himself). Although much was expected of the film (the Royal Philharmonic Orchestra were also involved), it seems to have been a commercial flop, even if perhaps Zappa himself considered it an artistic triumph. Ringo also attempted (with some success) to improve his songwriting while waiting for something to happen, but the most staggering news came during February, when it was disclosed by Allen Klein that The Beatles' income during 1970 had been more than four million pounds (of which Klein himself reputedly took a million and a half as commission), and that their income since he had become involved with their management had exceeded nine million pounds, which was rather more than they had earned during the previous seven years, although excluding songwriting royalties. On March 12, 1971, Paul's lawsuit to dissolve the Beatles' partnership was heard in court, and a receiver was appointed, although Klein remained involved with the group for some time.

John and Yoko recorded a new single in New York during February, with Phil Spector again producing the A side, *Power To The People*, a typically militant and somewhat ill-considered song of the type that had alerted the security watchdogs in America. John's clenched fist stance on the picture sleeve, wearing a combat helmet with oriental symbols on it, added to their paranoia, although at this point, there seemed to be little action that could be taken without alerting the media in a way which could ultimately be detrimental. The B side, yet another of Yoko's compositions, was deemed too offensive to be released in America, while its British release was delayed for a week as the lyrics to the song, *Open Your Box*, were considered distasteful by EMI Records (who continued to release Beatles material, although it usually bore an Apple Records label) and had to be altered. The record was felt by many to be over-repetitive, with the result that it rose no higher than Number Six in the British charts, and just failed to make the U.S. Top Ten.

In April, Ringo released his first solo single in Britain (it was his second in America, where the title track of *Beaucoups Of Blues* had been a minor hit). Ringo had written *It Don't Come Easy* himself, and with help from George (who produced it and played guitar), Stephen Stills, a notable American musician who around this time purchased Ringo's

Another shot of Ringo as Frank Zappa in '200 Motels'. Zappa also played himself in the film.

country house at Elstead, near Guildford in Surrey, and Klaus Voorman, who was popularly supposed to be on the verge of replacing Paul in the Beatles, the single was a great success, apparently outselling singles by each of the other Beatles on the market at the same time. It reached Number Four on both sides of the Atlantic, and restored the faith of many fans who might have viewed their purchases of Ringo's first two LPs as a waste of money. The month after it was released, Ringo and Maureen, along with Paul and Linda, were guests at the wedding of Mick Jagger to his first wife, Bianca, in St Tropez, and about a week later, the album Paul had been working on since the beginning of the year, *Ram*, was released. Everybody seemed to agree that it was a distinct improvement on its predecessor, and it reached Number Two in the LP charts of both Britain and America, while an excerpted single released in America, *Uncle Albert/Admiral Halsey*, was a million selling chart topper, although it was not released in single form in Britain, where the LP's final track, *The Back Seat Of My Car*, was released almost as an afterthought three months after the LP and became a very minor hit.

George, meanwhile, along with the renovation work and his Hare Krishna

immediately returned with her to America, while John and Yoko pondered what they could do next. They were instructed by a lawyer that the best thing to do would be to try to obtain an order for custody from the court in which Tony and Yoko's divorce had been heard, which was in the Virgin Islands. They acted on this advice, and Yoko was awarded custody.

There was a hiatus in this activity during the summer, while John in particular involved himself in New York culture and counter-culture, the main musical event coming in early June, when he and Yoko took the stage unannounced during a concert at the Fillmore East auditorium with the Mothers Of Invention, with whom Ringo had been involved earlier in the year for the '200 Motels' movie. Most of what was played that night (if the evidence of a live recording released the following year is any guide) was unintelligible, although John's version of a song he used to perform at The Cavern, *Well*, (in fact the B side to *Western Movies* by the Olympics, a 1958 hit), is at least a real song, which is more than can be said for the other three items, *Jamrag*, *Scumbag* and *Aü*. The live recordings of this 'event' later became part of a double album, *Some Time In New York City* but this was not released until more than a year after the event. A more immediate Lennon-connected release was *God Save Us/Do The Oz*, a single intended to raise

Above: Ringo and Maureen about to board a plane for St. Tropez, where they attended Mick Jagger's wedding in May, 1971.

Right: A scene from Mick and Bianca Jagger's celebrity-packed wedding with bride (left) and groom (right).

involvement, was also busy with a film documentary about his idol Ravi Shankar, 'Raga', in which he appeared, while John and Yoko were pursuing Kyoko with the utmost diligence. The relationship between the Lennons and Tony Cox, Kyoko's father, had been amicable initially, but Cox felt that he would rather remove his daughter from the disruption caused by public exposure, and rented a villa in Majorca where he tried to keep their presence and identity secret. However, Yoko discovered where Kyoko was and took her away from her father to the hotel where she and John were staying. Cox informed the police, who soon found Kyoko, whereupon the child, her estranged parents and Lennon were called together before a local magistrate, and Kyoko was asked whether she would prefer to live with her mother or her father. When the little girl chose Cox, he

money to help the proprietors of 'Oz' magazine, an 'underground' publication that was very popular with the hippie movement of the late 1960s and early 1970s, to fight a prosecution under the Obscene Publications Act. Lennon himself is not mentioned other than as writer and producer of the record, which is credited to the Elastic Oz Band, and this may have prevented it from becoming any more than a very minor hit.

After returning from America, John began work on his next LP, the basic tracks for which were recorded at his Ascot mansion. By this time, he had heard Paul's *Ram* album, and apparently considered two of the tracks, *Too Many People* and *Dear Boy*, to be vindictive personal attacks on him. Listening to the tracks, both might be regarded as reproving shakes of head at destroying some unspecified enterprise that had taken a

long time to establish – in *Too Many People*, the line 'You took your lucky break and broke it in two' recurs, while *Dear Boy* could be interpreted as a patronizing slap on the hand – but McCartney himself seems to have neither confirmed nor denied any concealed motive behind the songs. Just how personally Lennon seems to have taken the songs became clear during an interview with a music weekly, when he accused Paul of wanting to take charge of The Beatles' affairs, and added that he felt that Paul's behaviour was costing all the group's members a lot of money. Perhaps with this in mind, he included on his new LP a song titled *How Do You Sleep*, which, perhaps unlike the *Ram* songs, pulled no punches and was plainly addressed at Paul, and seemed to accuse him, among other things, of being unduly influenced by Linda and of making muzak (the type of music heard in

Above: John serenades Yoko on the white grand piano at Tittenhurst Park.

hotel reception areas and similar places, which generally makes no impression at all on those who hear it). Another track, *Crippled Inside*, was also supposedly directed at Paul, apparently in retaliation for *3 Legs*, another *Ram* track, but in neither case was the accusation plainly directed from Paul to John or vice versa, unless the listener mentally added details neither song actually contained.

While John was recording through the summer, George had conceived a plan for an all-star benefit concert to pour money into the disaster area of Bangla Desh, a province in the northeast of the Indian sub-continent that was involved in a bitter independence dispute with Pakistan, as a result of which many thousands of refugees were deprived and starving. Among those who agreed to appear were Eric Clapton, Billy Preston, Leon Russell and more than a dozen other musicians, many of whom had worked with George on *All Things Must Pass*, plus Bob Dylan. Getting Dylan to appear was a major coup, although had George managed to re-form The Beatles for the occasion, even Dylan's acquisition would have been dwarfed. George did in fact speak to his three erstwhile colleagues, and Ringo was pleased to appear, although John and Paul were conspicuous by their absence. Paul reportedly said that he would appear if George agreed to dissolve The Beatles' partnership, but inevitably the response was negative, while John actually went to New York fully intending to get on stage, until he asked what Yoko would be able to do, and, according to John Blake's 'All You Needed Was Love', was told that

Right: Sleeve to The Concert for Bangla Desh, *the triple LP of the concert staged by George to help the nation's starving refugees.*

George wanted her to enjoy watching the show. Predictably, Yoko was upset, and John eventually returned to England without even seeing the concert. Not that John's presence or otherwise could have affected the success of the event – two concerts took place on the first day of August, one during the afternoon and the other in the evening, which were recorded by the ubiquitous Phil Spector and also filmed. Each show played to a totally sold out audience of 20,000 people, who watched a set from Ravi Shankar, followed by an extended performance by the all star band, with individual showcases for Billy Preston, who sang his hit, *That's The Way God Planned It*, which George had produced, Ringo, who performed *It Don't Come Easy* (although on the evidence of the released live recording, he was uncertain of the words, even though it was his own song) and Leon Russell. The climax of the show came when all but George, Ringo and Leon Russell left the stage, and Bob Dylan was introduced for a twenty-minute, five-song set, before everyone returned for two more tracks sung by George, *Something*, from the *Abbey Road* album, and a track released as a single the day before, *Bangla Desh*. Musically, the concert was a huge success, and door receipts of just under a quarter of a million dollars were sent to the charity organization UNICEF a few days later, while considerably more money was expected from sales of the record and the film, although, as it happened, things didn't turn out quite the way everyone expected.

During July, the first Beatles LP since *Let It Be* was released in Britain – under the title *The Early Years*, it included all eight tracks recorded in Germany with Tony Sheridan ten years earlier, plus four other songs recorded by Sheridan, but with another backing band, from the same period. The album had been released before, in 1967, but because it seemed possible that there might be no more new Beatle records, the reissue attracted a little more attention with its new sleeve (featuring the issue of 'Mersey Beat' with The Beatles on the cover) than in previous incarnations. It was a timely reminder of the way things had once been, for in September, John and Yoko flew to America to continue their search for Kyoko. Having gained a custody order

from the Virgin Islands, they intended to simply collect the child and take her with them on their travels. Tony Cox was understandably apprehensive about the effect this might have on his daughter, and moved with Kyoko and his new wife to Houston, Texas, where the family set up home and Kyoko's name was changed to Rosemary. To further complicate matters, Cox had become a born-again Christian, but he and his wife were given temporary custody of Kyoko/Rosemary by a Houston court, although Yoko was permitted access to the child after paying a substantial sum to the court as a bond. Later in the year, this neo-soap opera would continue.

Above: George (left) and Bob Dylan on stage at Madison Square Garden for the Bangla Desh concert.

Left: Sleeve of The Early Years. *The LP, containing early tracks cut by the Beatles in Hamburg a decade earlier, was reissued with fresh packaging.*

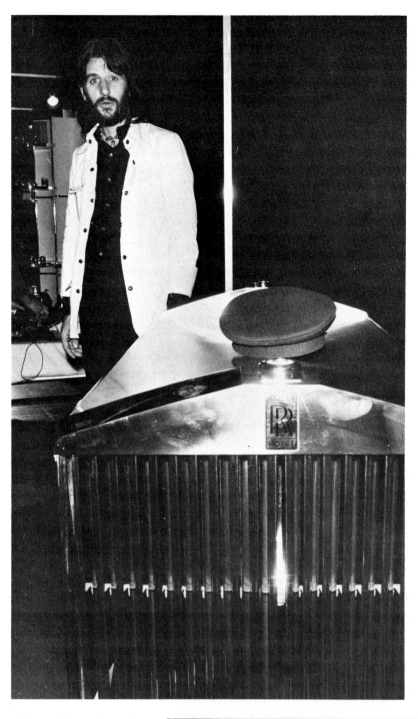

Paul McCartney was pleased with the success of *Ram*, and was looking forward to some success with the single from it that was about to be released in America, *Uncle Albert/Admiral Halsey*, but he still had a strong desire to play on stage again – the nearest he had been since The Beatles stopped touring was on the roof of the Apple building when they had performed *Get Back*. The sessions for *Ram* had been enjoyable, so Paul invited Denny Seiwell to become his permanent drummer, and Seiwell immediately agreed – who would be foolish enough to turn down a job with Paul McCartney? Another early recruit was Denny Laine, whom Paul had known when he was the main songwriter for Birmingham group, The Moody Blues. Laine had sung lead on the first and biggest hit by the Moodies (as they were known), *Go Now*, but after their initial popularity had begun to wane a year or two later, he had decided to leave the band, although they were at the time managed, ironically, by Brian Epstein. That was in late 1966, and Denny then spent two years getting nowhere fast, although an ambitious project he had evolved in the shape of a group known as the Electric String Band had released an acclaimed single around 1967, *Say You Don't Mind*, which Laine had also written. When Paul's invitation came, Denny had spent six months preparing songs for a solo album which he hoped someone would be prepared to finance. He was apparently sleeping on the floor of an office, and needed no second thoughts about the opportunity he had been offered.

Above: Ringo pictured at Regent Street store Liberty's in 1971, where an exhibition of his steel designs was displayed. A major talking point of the exhibition was the coffee table with a Rolls-Royce radiator at either end.

Right: John's Imagine *LP.*

Far right: Paul's Ram *album. Both it and* Imagine *were released in 1971.*

Linda was also going to be in the new group, although she had just had her third child, Stella, in September 1971, and it was she who suggested a name for the band – Wings. As soon as it was feasible, Paul booked time in a London recording studio, and with Tony Clarke (coincidentally the man who had worked with The Moody Blues after Denny Laine's departure from the group) producing, an album was completed at some speed with the title *Wild Life*, its sleeve picture showing the new band posing by a river in which Paul was standing while his three comrades sat on a branch of an overhanging tree with their feet in the water.

In September, John and Yoko resumed their struggle for Kyoko. It had been agreed that she should spend a weekend with them at her father's house preparatory to a ten-day stay with the Lennons over Christmas, but Cox refused to allow Kyoko to be left alone with the Lennons, who called in their highly paid lawyers and had him put in prison for contempt of court. This train of events actually took almost three months to unfold at the end of 1971. Interwoven with the Kyoko saga were musical matters – in early October, the LP which John had recorded during the summer at Ascot, *Imagine*, was released. Everyone agreed it was the masterpiece that had always been expected from John, and it largely compensated for the excesses of the three experimental albums, the live LP from Toronto and the primal therapy record, Lennon's previous LP offerings. The title track, in particular, would eventually be regarded as John's finest solo recording, but the rest of the record, as well as its packaging, was exceedingly controversial. John, having the impression that parts of Paul's *Ram* LP were directed at him, had replied in kind. The sleeve photograph of *Ram* shows Paul holding a ram by the horns (not as contrived a picture as might be imagined, since Paul did own a farm in Scotland), and Lennon's response was the postcard included in the album, which showed him holding a pig by the ears. Aside from the less subtle digs, *Imagine* included a number of excellent songs.

Even before it was released, John and Yoko had been busy with fresh musical projects. Yoko had recorded her own double album, *Fly*, around the time of the *Imagine* sessions, and a single from it,

Mrs. Lennon/Midsummer New York, was released during October, but failed to attract much attention. Also during October, John and Yoko went into a New York recording studio, The Record Plant, with Phil Spector, to make a Christmas single. Spector, of course, had been responsible for perhaps the finest Christmas LP of the rock'n'roll era, the quite classic *A Christmas Gift For You*, which featured the acts signed to his label, Philles Records, in 1963, including The Ronettes, The Crystals, Bob B. Soxx and the Blue Jeans and Darlene Love. While it was (and is) undoubtedly a masterpiece, it was initially released in the United States around the time of President Kennedy's

Above: Linda McCartney, pictured soon after joining her husband's group, Wings.

assassination, as a result of which it was overlooked in the general turmoil surrounding that world shattering event. Subsequently, it has been reissued and become acclaimed, but Spector was probably still dismayed that his finest moment (or at least one of them) had been ignored, and when the opportunity arose to make another Yuletide classic, he was eager to be involved. However, unlike many of his recent records with John and George, Spector wanted to revert to his celebrated 'Wall Of Sound' technique, which he used to great effect on *Happy Xmas* (*War Is Over*), the song he recorded with John and Yoko. Although the single obviously rivals the brilliance of the tracks on his original Christmas LP, it curiously failed to become an American hit in 1971, and in fact has never reached the American Top 40. In contrast, *Happy Xmas* has been a hit single in Britain on no less than five occasions, although not in 1971, when its release was postponed (for a year, since it refers to a specific time of year) due to the unwillingness of Northern Songs (who were still John's music publishers, despite the fact that he would probably have preferred them not to be) to accept that Yoko (whose songs were published by someone else) had co-written *Happy Xmas*.

The *Imagine* LP was released in the United States in September, 1971, and had sold more than a million copies by the time it was released in Britain, while the title track was released as a single in America, peaking at Number Three, whereas no British single was excerpted from the album at that time, although with the LP topping the charts on both sides of the Atlantic, it could be conceded that there was little point in releasing a single at all. And what of George and Ringo during the second half of 1971? Ringo was working on a new movie, a Spanish 'spaghetti Western' titled 'Blindman', in which he co-starred with one Tony Anthony (a Spaniard, of course). Ringo's was a non-musical role, and although concrete information about this non-Oscar award winning film is scarce, he was apparently a reasonably convincing villain. George, meanwhile, was discovering that even the best intentions can fall foul of profit-seeking record executives – although finally all the record companies who had the stars of the Bangla Desh Concerts under contract reluctantly agreed to allow their properties to appear on the live album that was planned, at the same time they insisted that the triple LP must be delayed until each label felt that it would not prejudice previously scheduled regular releases by their stars. In addition, George's plans to repeat the star-studded event in London and perhaps other large cities around the world were suddenly shattered when he discovered that anything he might earn, even though it was intended as a charitable donation, was liable to tax – in fact, when the American Internal Revenue Service learned that as much as twenty million dollars might accumulate in record and film income plus the various subsidiary rights, it decreed that virtually all the money must be kept untouched in a frozen account until they could assess the tax liability the event had attracted. Nevertheless, George went ahead with the release of the triple boxed set of the concerts, and eventually, the film, which reportedly jointly grossed over fifteen million dollars. Unfortunately for many of the refugees in Bangla Desh, the money arrived too late to keep them alive, and only a comparatively small percentage of that figure was left after taxation and other expenses. It was a bitter blow for George, understandably, after he had tried to do his best to assist what was undeniably a good cause.

The coda to John and Yoko's attempts to gain custody of Kyoko came at Christmas, just after the *Happy Xmas* single was released. Tony Cox was released from prison on the day after his arrest after a surety had been posted with the court that had incarcerated him, and immediately, he and his wife Melanie spirited Kyoko away to a secret destination. The Lennons hired private detectives to search for the Cox family, but they had obviously covered their tracks so effectively that they were not traced before it became clear even to John and Yoko that their actions were not only alienating the child, they were also terrifying her, and the hunt was called off, although it continued well into 1972.

Even before the eventful year had ended, John and Yoko found themselves involved in another 'cause' – soon after they arrived in New York, John became involved in the frantic life of Greenwich Village, and was soon identified by the radical element as a means by which issues could be publicized simply because one of The Beatles was involved in them. Sometimes, this type of activity was successful (if that is the correct word), as in the case of John and Yoko appearing at a demonstration organized by the radical youth of America to protest the imprisonment of White Panther leader and political activist John Sinclair for ten years for possession of a fairly small quantity of marijuana – John's presence at the protest meeting

Above: A menacing Ringo threatens the cameraman in another 'Blindman' still.

attracted maximum publicity, and soon afterwards, Sinclair was freed. This was by no means the sole involvement of the Lennons in similar 'causes'.

Paul McCartney had different problems. After the burst of enthusiasm during which he had formed Wings and quickly recorded the *Wild Life* album, the LP was released in early December to almost unanimous media criticism, which in Britain at least was also reflected in its performance in chart terms, although it eventually sold enough to be certified gold, largely on the strength of bigger sales to a less-discriminating American public. In many ways, it was a good thing that 1971 was over, as more had happened that was negative than positive, although Ringo was reasonably content, and both John and Paul were convinced that they were making some progress towards a happier future. If they had been able to accurately predict at the start of 1972 how they would feel at the end of the year, each of the erstwhile Beatles (with the possible exception of Ringo) might have preferred to pass the time in some kind of hibernation.

Looking back on their activities during 1972, the year seems to have been far less frantic than the one it followed. This is certainly true in terms of record releases as only John completed an album (albeit a double) and George was conspicuous by his absence from the new release

125

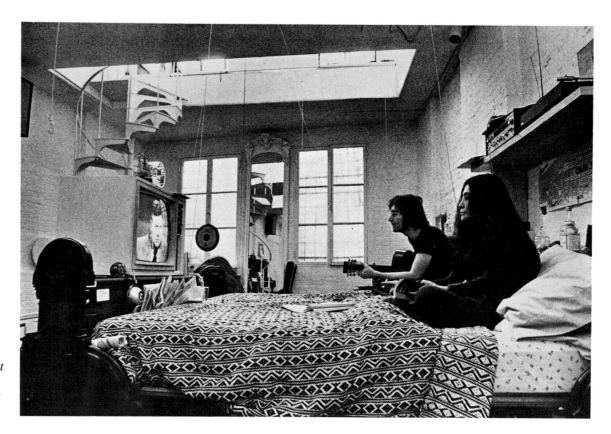

Right: John and Yoko at home in their Greenwich village apartment during the early 1970s.

schedules, leaving aside the *Bangla Desh* set, which actually appeared in Britain during the first week of the year, several weeks after its U.S. release before Christmas 1971. There were, however, pressing problems for each of The Beatles during the year, several of which reached a ghastly climax.

John Lennon's continuing involvement with the anti-establishment reached several crisis points. After his protests on behalf of John Sinclair, he and Yoko were also prevailed upon to add their considerable weight (in publicity terms) to the burgeoning civil rights movement highlighting the plight of the American Indians who were being restricted to smaller and smaller reservations with a resultant decline in the quality of their ethnic culture. Of more immediate concern to the forces of law and order in the U.S.A., however, were his protests (along with those of innumerable others) about the bloody riot at Attica State Prison in New York, which resulted in the deaths of 28 inmates after troops opened fire on the rioters. This unhappy event had taken place on September 13, 1971, after which a growing swell of public condemnation was rising to fever pitch. It was an obvious cause in which John could become involved, but his antipathy towards the status quo in America was a matter of concern for the internal security agencies

in America – not only did he attract maximum publicity because of his position as a celebrity, he seemed to have the ability to influence American youth to an almost frightening extent. He had already been the subject of a secret memorandum in early 1971, but a year later, as his activities escalated, he was regarded as a positive threat. Fate came to the aid of the U.S. security services during February 1972, when it transpired that John's temporary resident visa (which permitted him to remain in America) was about to expire. When he tried to extend the visa (little suspecting that he was the subject of intense government scrutiny), his application was refused, the reason given being that he had been convicted of drug use in London during October 1968 – this was when Yoko was pregnant, but lost the baby largely due to the intense turmoil surrounding the case. The fact that the policeman who had organized the prosecution had subsequently been convicted himself of planting drugs on suspects (something John had at the time hinted at, although he had been unwilling to start an outcry due to Yoko's fragile condition) was conveniently ignored.

John probably did little to provoke public sympathy for his plight when he and Yoko appeared on a nationally networked TV show during February, after which he was told that he and his wife

Denny Laine was evidently viewed as a rhythm player/vocalist rather than a soloist – who turned out to be Henry McCullough. He was a very experienced musician whose track record included work with Joe Cocker's Grease Band (which he continued to front after Cocker left – among their best-known but least acknowledged work was the original *Jesus Christ Superstar* album, which sold several million copies). McCullough was at somewhat of a loose end at the start of 1972, and was as pleased as Denny Laine had been to work with Paul, although neither was apparently very enthusiastic that the keyboard player with Wings was Linda McCartney, who was very much a beginner as a musician. During the first week in February, the organizers of student entertainment at Nottingham University were surprised to receive a phone call from someone who asked whether it would be possible for Wings to

Left: Linda McCartney on stage with Wings in 1972.

Below: John Lennon during a rare live appearance in the 1970s.

must leave the United States by mid-March. Apart from anything else, this meant that John had to abandon his plans to tour with a New York rock group known as Elephant's Memory. However, the group would not only appear on Lennon's next album release, but also were accorded the almost unique privilege of having their own LP produced by John and Yoko. More important, of course, was the threat to his freedom of access to the United States – when John had left England during the autumn of 1972, it is generally felt that he intended to return at some point, although in fact he was fated never to set foot in Britain again. While he had apparently made no plans to visit Britain, the saga of Kyoko was still an active concern, and the refusal to renew his visa effectively meant that he was unable to leave the U.S.A. for fear that he would not be allowed to return. At least while he was in America, he could fight his deportation from a position of comparative strength.

Paul McCartney had bounced back from the critical tirade that had greeted the release of the *Wild Life* LP, and was keen to prove the critics wrong by touring with Wings, although he was adamant that his return to the live concert stage must not be surrounded by a huge publicity campaign. The first step was to recruit a guitarist to complete the group –

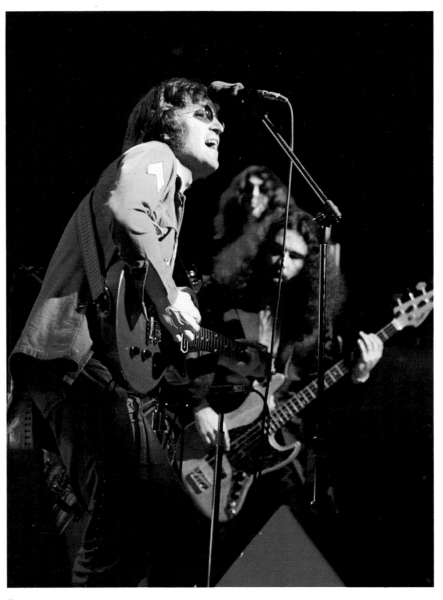

Right: An early line up of Wings featuring (from left) Denny Seiwell, Linda and Paul McCartney, Denny Laine and Henry McCullough.

Above: Paul (right) and Henry McCullough on stage with Wings in 1972.

play a concert at the college on the following day. Since they had nothing to lose (and perhaps plenty to gain) by agreeing, the college authorities were happy to allow the world debut of Wings as a live group to take place on their property, and a series of 'ad hoc' concerts lasting two weeks and held at various colleges around Britain gave the new group a relatively gentle introduction to live work. The tour ended at about the time a new single by Paul (but credited to Wings, of course) was released.

If he had been hoping to curry favour with the critics after the débâcle of *Wild Life*, *Give Ireland Back To The Irish* was destined to be of little benefit, although, in fairness, it seems most unlikely that his motive for making the record had anything to do with the critics, as it plainly referred to an incident that had occurred during the previous month (January 1972) when 13 civilians were killed by troops during a riot resulting from a banned civil rights march in Londonderry

While this incident was typical of the confusion and destruction produced by civil war (and became known as 'Bloody Sunday'), Paul's single was immediately banned from the airwaves in Britain. Of course, the supposed 'banning' of a record (the truth is more frequently that radio producers are almost never prevented from playing a record unless it is flagrantly indecent or obviously offensive, but their good taste is relied upon to omit such items) inevitably results in a publicity build up, as was the case with *Give Ireland Back To The Irish*, which reached the Top 20 in Britain and the Top 30 in America. Later in the year, John Lennon's *Sometime In New York City* album would include a track titled *Sunday Bloody Sunday* on a similar, if more specific, subject.

Ringo Starr was probably able to look back on 1971 as a fairly satisfactory year,

although he was experiencing some marital problems. His wife Maureen was less exotic than Yoko, less patrician than Linda and less famous than Patti – Maureen might have made an ideal wife for any of the other Beatles, since she was ultimately loyal to Ringo, and brought up their children to be as normal as possible considering that their father was such a celebrity. She would also reputedly make sure that Ringo came home to a cooked meal every evening, and although she sometimes accompanied him on night-clubbing excursions to late-night London, apparently preferred to stay at home with the kids, although she was desperately lonely as the lady of a large house with virtually no neighbours for miles. Nevertheless, she was obviously pleased that Ringo had achieved such a big hit with *It Don't Come Easy*, and that he appeared to be making some headway towards breaking into the film world. Ringo's second British single, *Back Off*

Boogaloo, was released in mid-March, and like its predecessor, was a big hit, reaching the Top Ten on both sides of the Atlantic. During the same month, Ringo also took his cinematic ambitions a step further, this time as producer and director of a semi-documentary titled 'Born To Boogie', which starred Marc Bolan and T. Rex, arguably the most popular British act of that period, who scored nine consecutive Top Three hits in Britain in the two and a half years from the autumn of 1970. Elton John also appeared in the film as a guest star, and at the time of its release, it was fairly popular with audiences.

John Lennon was still struggling against deportation, so after his visa expired, he and Yoko presented themselves to the Immigration authorities accompanied by their lawyer, who apparently argued most forcibly that to expel Lennon would merely be to repeat a previous mistake made by the authorities, when they expelled the famous film star, Charlie Chaplin. Although it didn't change the minds of the immigration officers, their lawyer's eloquence at least provided a stay of execution for John and Yoko during which an appeal could be prepared, something that had previously been prohibited. It was probably not the smartest of moves to release almost simultaneously a new single with the inflammatory title of *Woman Is The Nigger Of The World*, a feminist preview of the forthcoming *Some Time In New York City* album, but since it was plainly an indifferent piece of music at

best, it attracted very little attention, either in the media or among record buyers, and failed to even make the U.S. Top 50. By the end of April, publicity surrounding Lennon's deportation had built the affair into a major issue, with various very prominent people protesting that the decision was unconstitutional – this band of defenders included the Mayor of New York, John Lindsay, Lord Harlech, one-time British ambassador to the United States, actors Tony Curtis and Jack Lemmon, a powerful Trade Union boss and several poets and painters of note. John was safe – for the moment – and allegedly met Paul in New York soon afterwards, where they apparently discussed their mutual disgust with the situation in Ireland. During their meeting, John is said to have indicated that he approved of Paul's gesture in releasing *Give Ireland Back To The Irish*.

During May, Paul released a follow-up single, which was even more unenthusiastically received by the critics. *Mary Had A Little Lamb* – the nursery rhyme recorded, so legend has it, because his daughter Mary, who was two years old at the time, enjoyed hearing her name being sung. Unfortunately, few others seemed to share her enthusiasm, although the record briefly featured in the Top Ten in Britain and was also a minor hit in America.

George emerged from seclusion, still unhappy about the fate of the millions he had earned for charity, but pleased to receive an award from UNICEF, which was presented to him by the Secretary-General of the United Nations, Kurt Waldheim, who also presented a similar award at the same ceremony to Ravi Shankar, who had first alerted George to the plight of the starving millions. However, the big news of the month for Beatle fanatics was the release of a new John Lennon LP, although perhaps inevitably, it was controversial, this time even before it was released – the album sleeve was designed to resemble a newspaper, with lyrics to the songs in the place of the articles and supposedly appropriate pictures completing the effect. One of the pictures, however, was cleverly airbrushed to show President Nixon and Chairman Mao apparently dancing together, both completely naked, and this led to a number of record shops refusing to stock

Above: Wings on their open-topped bus during their 1972 European tour.

the album until the picture was covered up. The music was hardly less provocative – songs about the Attica Prison Riot, John Sinclair, Angela Davis (on trial at the time for conspiring to help her husband, George Jackson, escape from prison), as well as two items protesting about British involvement in Northern Ireland, *The Luck Of The Irish* and *Sunday Bloody Sunday*. The package also included a so-called 'free' LP, one side of which had been recorded two years earlier at the UNICEF concert presented in London when the Plastic Ono Band concept had been fresh, and the other recorded the previous year when John and Yoko had appeared with Frank Zappa and the Mothers of Invention.

Paul McCartney was still certain that touring held the answer to his problems, and arranged for Wings to embark on a tour of Europe. The party had been on the road for more than a month before anything out of the ordinary occurred. Then, in Gothenburg, Sweden, the local police intercepted a parcel addressed to the hotel at which the group were staying, and Paul, Linda and Denny Seiwell were held for

questioning, although they were eventually released after paying a fine of around £1000. Unfortunately for the McCartneys, despite the fact that they had evidently escaped lightly, the story was widely reported in newspapers in many countries, and this probably resulted in another drug bust later in the year.

Ringo, still deservedly pleased with himself after a second big hit single and the Marc Bolan movie, was furthering his cinematic endeavours by working with noted American singer/songwriter Harry Nilsson on a comedy spoof of the classic horror film, titled 'Son Of Dracula'. While it would be unfair to condemn the film out of hand without having seen it, the consensus of opinion appears to be that it wasn't a great success, although Ringo's friendship with Nilsson (which had begun earlier in the year when he drummed on the latter's *Son Of Schmilsson* LP) would turn out to be very significant. During the following month of September, Ringo was involved in another major project, although this time as a guest singer. 'Tommy', the 'rock opera' written mainly by Pete Townshend of

The Who, was being re-recorded with an all-star cast assisting The Who, and among the guests making cameo appearances were Rod Stewart, Stevie Winwood, Richie Havens and actor Richard Harris, while Ringo performed two songs, *Fiddle About* and *Tommy's Holiday Camp*, which were originally sung by his drumming counterpart in The Who, Keith Moon. Otherwise, the rest of Ringo's year was fairly quiet, and much the same could be said for George Harrison.

In fact, aside from John and Yoko showing their gratitude to Mayor Lindsay for his support in their fight against deportation, by appearing at a benefit concert in aid of the 'One To One' project aimed at helping backward children, which was a great success, the major spotlight of the final four months of 1972 fell on Paul. On his return from the European tour, he was surprised to discover that news of the Swedish drug case had excited the curiosity of the local policeman, who had apparently returned from a course on drug identification and whose territory included Paul's Scottish farm. While checking that the farm was secure while the McCartneys were away, the policeman had come across a crop of marijuana plants in a greenhouse. Paul was fined £100 for cultivation, and it has been postulated that the next Wings single, released at the beginning of December, was some kind of reaction to this 'persecution' concerning his smoking habits. Its title – *Hi Hi Hi* – might lead to suspicions that the suggestions were accurate, but its inability to get as much radio play as a new Paul McCartney single might expect seems to have been more due to what was seen as its suggestiveness in sexual terms. In fact, the song's simple lyric was no more or less suggestive than any number of blues songs that were and are played freely over the airwaves, and it can only be presumed that extra sensitivity existed among radio programmers where Paul was concerned in view of his brushes with the law in previous months. Despite the limited airplay, the single (whose B side, *C Moon*, a reggae-flavoured song, was as good as *Hi Hi Hi* and also eminently playable) became Paul's biggest British hit single with Wings thus far, and also reached the American Top Ten. No doubt it was some consolation after such a difficult year.

Above: Ringo (centre) filming Marc Bolan at Wembley for 'Born To Boogie'.

Left: Ringo during the early 1970s.

133

Exploding the Myth (1973-1976)

The major activity at the start of 1973 came from the Lennons, whose *Happy Xmas (War Is Over)* single had finally been released in Britain, and stood at Number Two in the charts at the beginning of January. John Lennon was still largely concerned with his fight against deportation, but this left Yoko time to record another solo album during the final weeks of 1972, which was released under the title of *Approximately Infinite Universe* early in the new year. No doubt because he was busy with his own problems, John took a smaller part than usual in his wife's second double LP – all the songs are credited to Yoko alone, while the backing was by Elephant's Memory with only token assistance from John, who is

Right: Ringo in a scene from 'That'll Be The Day', in which his acting as a teddy boy was widely acclaimed.

credited where he appears instrumentally as 'Joel Nohnn' (his name consisted of too many 'n's for more than a poor anagram). However, he is listed as co-producer with Yoko, but just as before, the record could hardly be termed a great success.

Ringo was also fairly active during this period, playing a 1950s teddy boy in the acclaimed movie 'That'll Be The Day' starring David Essex. When the film was released in February, Ringo was universally praised for the authenticity he brought to this evocation of the early days of British holiday camps, while David Essex, of course, went on to many more triumphs, both as singer and actor. Paul seemed to have finally exorcized the previous year's problems with the release of *My Love*, a tuneful single that sounded like a very obvious hit, which it was, topping the U.S. charts and reaching the Top Ten in Britain. It was a trailer for his upcoming *Red Rose Speedway* LP, and was credited, perhaps in deference to suggestions by EMI's marketing experts, to 'Paul McCartney & Wings'. Nevertheless, Paul was seemingly still fascinated with the possibility of preventing others from experiencing his traumas of 1972, and played a benefit concert for 'Release', an organization founded to help those with legal and other problems connected with drug taking. Wings were also in the studio during the first three months of 1973, making their new LP.

At the end of March, Allen Klein's term as manager of The Beatles ended when Klein's company, ABKCO Inc, decided not to renew its contract with John, George and Ringo, although inevitably a series of law suits over the division of money would drag on for some considerable time, and would eventually cost The Beatles a small matter of five million

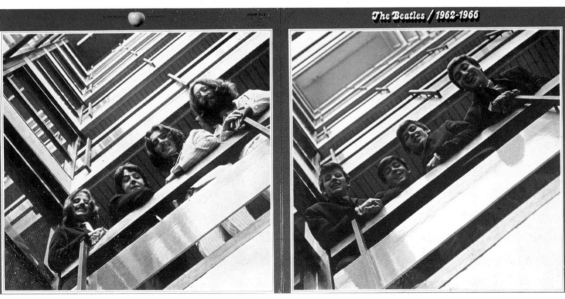

dollars. This was followed soon afterwards by the release of two double albums of reissued Beatles material, titled *1962–1966* and *1967–1970*, which sold prodigiously on both sides of the Atlantic, although nothing new was included of any sort. Perhaps the solo efforts had resulted in the infinitely superior group records

being recalled so often that many people took the opportunity to buy a well-chosen selection of Beatle favourites when they became available, but the reissues appear to have been conceived as a direct result of an unauthorized four-LP set titled *The Beatles Alpha Omega*, being released in America, and causing great interest. The official double albums were amazingly successful, both of them reaching the Top Three of the LP charts on both sides of the Atlantic. Perhaps it was this new excitement about his previous group that helped Paul McCartney's new Wings LP, *Red Rose Speedway*, to become a big hit in the United States, and a reasonable success in Britain, since the album, despite the inclusion of *My Love*,

Below: A slightly contrived shot of the second line up of Wings, apparently crossing the Sahara desert. (Left to right foreground) Denny Seiwell, Paul, Linda, Denny Laine and Henry McCullough.

recorded a song with Wings plus a full orchestra, with George Martin producing and arranging it. The song was subsequently submitted to the producers of the latest in the series of 'James Bond' films, 'Live And Let Die', and was selected as the title song, and predictably it became a major success, as do most Bond movie themes. In addition, Martin won a Grammy Award for his arrangement.

George Harrison emerged from virtual isolation towards the middle of the year, releasing his first single for nearly two years, *Give Me Love (Give Me Peace On Earth)*, which was also included on his *Living In The Material World* LP, released shortly afterwards. The 45 was fairly successful, actually topping the American chart for a week, a feat the LP improved upon, staying at Number One for more than a month. In Britain, however, after an early flurry of buying – this was, after all, the follow-up to either *All Things Must Pass* or the *Bangla Desh* set, or both – the LP quickly vanished from the charts after it became clear that George's religious beliefs were the inspir-

Right: A still from 'James Paul McCartney', the TV Special.

was hardly earth-shattering. It also enjoyed the distinction of becoming the first Wings LP that the band promoted via a full-scale British tour, while there was still more activity in the McCartney camp with the making and screening (to predictably mixed reaction) of a TV Special titled 'James Paul McCartney'. Paul also

ation behind many of the songs, which were actually rather boring. The long-term effect in Britain was that George's records thereafter were treated with great suspicion, and he has never (to the time of writing) appeared in the Top 20 of either the British singles or albums chart subsequently with a solo recording.

In terms of recording success among the ex-Beatles, the year definitely belonged to Ringo. It all started, according to record producer Richard Perry, when Harry Nilsson was invited to be a guest presenter at the Grammy Award ceremony. Nilsson was not keen to oblige, but Perry sensed that if he could persuade Ringo to accomany him, Nilsson might agree, which was exactly what transpired. However, prior to this, Richard Perry had suggested to Ringo that he should make a new solo LP which the former would produce, and after the Grammy Awards were over, Ringo took Perry up on his offer. As luck would have it, both John Lennon and George Harrison were in Los Angeles (where Perry owns a recording studio), and after a meeting to discuss the latest problems with the Allen Klein situation, Ringo played the tracks he had recorded to John – George had already been contributing, both as a songwriter and a musician, on the sessions – who became very excited and immediately wrote a song for Ringo to sing on the LP titled *I'm The Greatest*. It was getting close to being a reunion of the Beatles, but of course Paul was absent. Due to his problems during the previous year over drug busts, he was at that time not allowed to enter the United States, despite numerous requests for visas. However, Paul subsequently invited Richard Perry to England to work on another project, and Perry, who was also using his time in Britain to complete work on Ringo's LP, was happy to be given a song written by Paul for Ringo to sing, on which both Paul and Linda appeared as backing singers. It was the nearest that the four Beatles would ever come to re-forming.

Despite his help for Ringo, Paul McCartney was experiencing difficulties with Wings. Both Denny Seiwell and Henry McCullough had been very happy to join the band, but Henry in particular was unhappy about Paul telling him what to play, and when Paul announced to the band that he intended to record the next Wings LP in Nigeria, Henry handed in his resignation, as did Seiwell a few days later. Unperturbed, Paul, Linda and Denny Laine set off for Lagos, to work in a studio

Below: Paul again at the piano in another scene from the 1973 TV spectacular titled 'James Paul McCartney'.

Right: John Lennon during the mid-1970s with May Pang, Yoko's secretary. John and May shared an affair when he and Yoko felt the need to live apart.

owned by English drummer Ginger Baker after first recording a new single, *Helen Wheels* (the name Paul gave to his Land Rover) to ensure that the trip would not be a fool's errand. The single wasn't a huge hit nor especially inspired, but it served the purpose of proving that a worthwhile record could be made without either a lead guitarist nor a specialist drummer.

Apart from his work with Ringo, John Lennon had been uncharacteristically quiet for most of 1973, and it transpired that the reason for this was that he was involved in a long and very unpleasant quarrel with Yoko, which initially resulted in him remaining in Los Angeles for some months after working with Ringo. During this time he supposedly engaged in an affair with Yoko's Japanese secretary, May Pang, to which Yoko apparently did not object, such was the breakdown in her relationship with John. However, there was to be one final instance of John and Yoko releasing albums on the same day – obviously, they still felt the need to present an apparently combined front to the world, although where Yoko's *Feeling The Space* was little dif-

ferent from her previous albums (with John playing guitar using the pseudonym of John O'Cean on a couple of tracks), John's *Mind Games* happily marked the end of his militant attitude towards what he saw as the oppression that existed in the world. It has been suggested that after the adverse reaction to *Some Time In New York City*, Lennon was trying to return to a musical path more generally acceptable – as he put it himself, 'An interim record between being a manic political lunatic and a musician'. Inevitably, the sloganeering wasn't quite absent – the final track on side one is 'Nutopian National Anthem' (actually a few seconds of complete silence), and the inner sleeve contains a 'Declaration Of Nutopia', which is described as 'a conceptual country with no land, no boundaries, no passports, only people, and no laws other than cosmic'. Since the 'track' would not be noticed by anyone unaware of its existence, this was a fairly futile gesture, and the same might be said of *Aisumasen (I'm Sorry)* (which mean the same thing in Japanese and English, respectively), and was supposedly addressed to Yoko by John on the

Left: Paul and Linda in 1973, modelling snow boots.

subject of their estrangement. Its apparent futility may be judged from the fact that they were still apart as the LPs were released. *Mind Games* was in fact by no means a disaster, largely due to the majesty of the title track, although its chart positions (26 in Britain, 18 in America) were comparatively modest. The LP was certified gold within a month of its release, and amid this success, John, in company with George and Ringo, also finally fell into agreement with Paul by instituting law suits against Allen Klein.

The surprise success of the year (at least to record buyers) was Ringo, whose only release in the previous eighteen months had been his small contributions to *Tommy*. During the autumn, the LP he had recorded with Richard Perry producing was previewed by the release of a single, *Photograph*, which reached the Top Ten in Britain and also became Ringo's first chart topping 45 in America. It was an excellent record, and when the album from which it came, simply titled *Ringo*, was released soon afterwards, it too made a substantial chart impact, as did a subsequent single, Ringo's version of

Left: Sleeve to the eponymous and highly successful 1973 LP by Ringo.

Johnny Burnette's teenage classic, *You're Sixteen*, which peaked at Number Four in both Britain and America. The obvious inference – that the presence of the other three Beatles on the album, albeit not all together, may have been noted by some record buyers – should not be dismissed as a reason for the great success, but to the credit of everyone involved, little appears to have been made of it in terms of publicity, and the record surely sold simply because it was extremely good.

Paul's LP mostly made in Nigeria was also somewhat of a revelation after the patchiness of his previous four post-Beatles albums. Despite the limited instrumentation of Wings at the time, the LP, *Band On The Run*, was certainly Paul's most perfectly realized solo album to date, and is felt by many to have been the pinnacle of his solo career even allowing for the many records that followed it. The album sleeve was as arresting as the music – Paul, Linda and Denny Laine, along with half a dozen personalities selected by Paul, were photographed wearing what appeared to be prison uniform and were caught in the glare of a spotlight as if they had just escaped from a penal institution. If that was eye catching, the music on the record was even more sensational, a sentiment with which the public evidently agreed – the LP topped the charts in Britain, where it remained on the LP chart for a year and a half, and America, where it featured in the Top 100 for nearly a year. Additionally, two singles taken from the LP, *Jet* and the title track, were big hits, and the *Band On The Run* single topped the US charts as well as winning a Grammy Award for 'Best Pop Vocal Performance By A Group' in 1974. All in all, 1973 was a very good year for Paul – not only had he now come up with an acclaimed masterpiece and triumphed over adversity when two vital members of Wings had flown away, he had his three ex-colleagues in agreement with him about Allen Klein. And to cap it all, an excellent Christmas present came with the news that his application for a visa to work

in America, which had been turned down on several previous occasions due to his 1972 drug convictions, had at last been granted.

The start of 1974 saw each of The Beatles at very different stages of their lives. Paul was as happy as at any time since the group split up four years previously and Ringo was on the crest of a wave of success which virtually no one could have anticipated, although his marriage was under pressure even more than usual due to his reaffirmed status as a major rock star. George's marriage was in even worse condition. His best friend Eric Clapton, now cured of his heroin addiction, was giving his attentions to Patti, who felt neglected as a result of George's religious affiliations. Patti retained a certain loyalty towards George where Eric was concerned – being cuckolded by your best friend is never a less than crushing experience. Perhaps George was too busy with his devotions to notice, but he was considerably more upset when his wife took on a modelling job very much against his wishes, and decided that he needed a holiday in India where he could consult with the various gurus to whom he had become attached.

John Lennon was, as ever, busy getting involved with enterprises he had not fully thought out before he embarked on them, although in fairness, his life was under considerable pressure on several fronts. He was still co-habiting with May Pang in Los Angeles, although it would seem that simultaneously he was in touch with Yoko, who remained in New York, as around this time, the Lennon household (albeit without John) moved into an apartment in the Dakota Building, a block notable for its stringent security aimed at keeping unwanted visitors away. John was still fighting to be allowed to remain in America, and his lawyer was appealing against everything to provide more time. While this was successful in that John was not forcibly deported, it was still a precarious existence, and among the steps John took was to write to Buckingham Palace asking for a Royal Pardon over his drug conviction. At the end of the year, he also made the decision to work on an album that displayed his rock'n'roll roots, composed of oldies he had enjoyed before The Beatles became so world-shatteringly successful. The scheme was an excellent

Right: Sleeve to Band On The Run, *the exceptional Wings LP released in 1973. From left, TV personality Michael Parkinson, singer/comedian Kenny Lynch, Paul, film star James Coburn, Linda (at front), Member of Parliament Clement Freud (behind Linda), actor Christopher Lee, Denny Laine, boxer John Conteh.*

Left: A 1974 photograph of John Lennon, taken in Los Angeles during his separation from Yoko.

Below: Another study of John Lennon from 1974. Both this and the picture above remained unseen until after Lennon's murder.

one, and to help him, John contacted Phil Spector, who was equally enthusiastic about the project, particularly when John told him that he wanted to be directed totally, as opposed to his previous projects with John where the latter would often overrule Spector's suggestions. Precisely what was recorded during the sessions is difficult to establish, as will become clear, but apparently at least fifteen completed songs resulted by the end of 1973. Both Spector and Lennon were apparently using a good deal of artificial assistance to help them through their work, and Spector was known to be unpredictable so that when he failed to arrive for sessions from time to time, John was not particularly worried, until it became clear after a lengthy absence that Spector wasn't returning to the studio at all. John enquired at Spector's fortress-like mansion, and was apparently told by a security guard that Spector had been involved in a motor-cycle accident and was extremely ill, which made it impossible for the tapes to be retrieved. A further complication was that Spector, without John's knowledge, had seemingly convinced Warner Brothers Records to pay for the studio time, although John was still contracted to Capitol Records in America. The situation evidently got so much on top of

A reflective Paul McCartney in the mid-1970s.

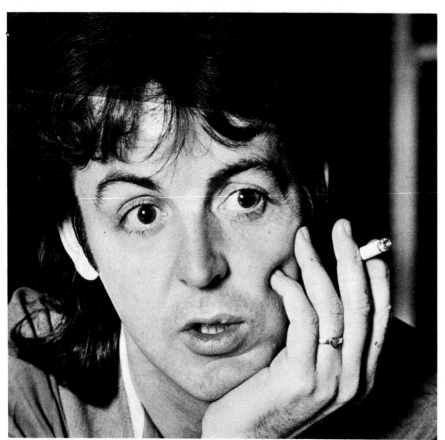

John, who was at the same time close to a reconciliation with Yoko, that he began drinking to excess, often in the company of Harry Nilsson.

The one constructive item to result from this activity was that John agreed to produce an album for Nilsson, along similar lines to the former's 'back to the roots' concept, which was in abeyance due to Spector's disappearance. Although an impressive number of star names took part in the making of this LP, including Ringo, Keith Moon of The Who, Klaus Voorman and a substantial number of notable American players, the results, when they were released later in the year under the title of *Pussycats*, were distinctly ordinary. The concept of recording oldies was only followed for half the album and nothing was a duplication of the tracks Lennon had recorded, but the rest of the songs were fairly ordinary originals by Nilsson (and in one case, John). John is not credited with singing or playing on the record, perhaps because he supposedly became aware at some point during the lengthy and exhausting sessions that Nilsson was very ill, probably due to various excesses, to the point where his once expressively excellent voice had dramatically deteriorated, whereupon John tried (with some success) to curb the destruction process. Not long after work on *Pussycats* was completed, John bade farewell to May Pang and returned to Yoko.

Paul, after the huge success of *Band On The Run*, was anxious to return to playing on stage, especially since he could now tour in America with his newly acquired visa. Of course, he needed to rebuild Wings before touring anywhere, so he held auditions for guitarists and drummers during April, eventually offering the posts to two British musicians, Geoff Britton and Jimmy McCulloch. Britton's most notable previous musical exploit had been with a well-known rock'n'roll revival group known as The Wild Angels, while McCulloch had first come to wide public notice as a member of a bizarre trio known as Thunderclap Newman, whose only LP included a chart topping British single titled *Something In The Air*. One problem that Paul had not foreseen was that the two new recruits hated the sight of each other, which made touring, and especially recording, a problem.

George Harrison emerged from hibernation in mid-year when he announced that he had formed his own record label, Dark Horse, although since he was still contractually tied to the EMI group, he would be unable to record for the label himself for at least two years. Inevitably, he announced that the first signing to the label would be Ravi Shankar, and coincidentally, another artist who appeared on Dark Horse some time later was Henry McCullough, the guitar player who had left Wings. George also announced that he was putting together a band with whom he intended to tour before the end of the year, and with whom he would be recording a new LP to coincide with the tour. Recording for the album took place at the studio George had constructed within Friar Park, and at virtually the same time, Ringo was in Los Angeles with Richard Perry, making a follow-up to the phenomenally successful *Ringo* LP. On this occasion, the only other ex-Beatle who helped out was John Lennon, who not only played on three tracks, but also wrote *Goodnight Vienna*, which was selected as the record's title song. Elton John also wrote a song for Ringo and played on it, and the effect seemed to be very similar to *Ringo*, although, of course, neither George (who was making his own record in England), nor Paul (who was rehearsing prior to touring) were available to lend a hand.

By June 1974, John Lennon was back in New York, and in the continuing absence of the tapes recorded with Phil Spector, he felt obliged to make a new LP, because it would be a year since the release of *Mind Games* before anything new could come out. The resulting album, *Walls And Bridges*, was by no means a masterpiece. It contained several songs written about Yoko, while the backing musicians included Elton John and Julian Lennon, John's son by his first marriage, who had taken up drums, and was allowed to play them on a short track completing the LP, *Ya Ya*. The commercial fate of the album was very different on the opposite sides of the Atlantic – in Britain, where the first 45 taken from the album, *Whatever Gets You Through The Night*, was only a small hit, the album briefly reached the Top Ten, but in America, both single and LP topped their respective charts. A second single taken from the album, *No.9 Dream*,

was equally a far bigger hit in the United States than in Britain.

In Britain, Paul and Wings released two singles within a week during October (they were almost a month apart in the U.S.A.), although one of them was released under the name of The Country Hams. This tune was one Paul's father had written several years before, titled *Walking In The Park With Eloise*, and was recorded in Nashville with the new Wings line-up augmented by notable country & Western stars Chet Atkins on guitar and Floyd Cramer on piano, their presence presumably being the inspiration for the name 'Country Hams'. Precisely what Paul expected of this single is difficult to say – there was no indication that he was involved, and as no one was made aware of the identity of the musicians, the single was almost totally ignored, although it was reissued during 1982 (by which time Paul's involvement was better known) but still failed to reach the chart. The official Wings single, *Junior's Farm*, inevitably sold rather better, although it was still the group's worst-placed single since *Give Ireland Back To The Irish* in Britain, whereas in America, even the flipside of the record, *Sally G*, became a Top 40 hit. This was actually a curious phenomenon – while *Junior's Farm* was originally con-

A somewhat happier pose from the same session.

Right: Sleeve to George's poorly received Dark Horse *LP, released in Britain a few days before Christmas 1974.*

Below: An apprehensive George Harrison on stage during the mid-1970s.

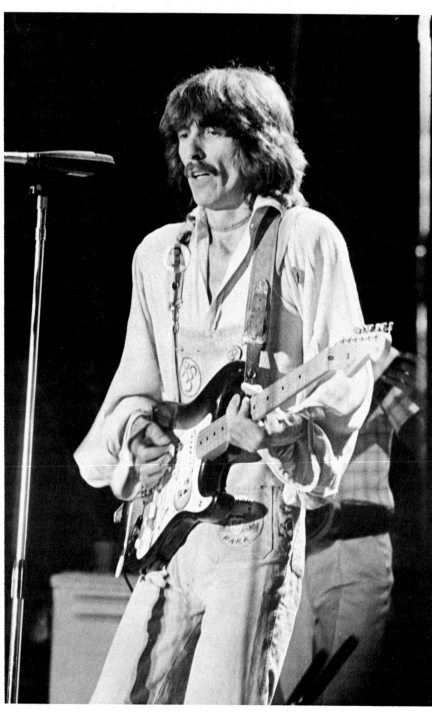

sidered to be the 'A' side of the disc, several months after it was released, the record was reissued with *Sally G* as the 'A' side and *Junior's Farm* relegated to subsidiary status. Not that there was any rule prohibiting such a course of action (which was largely fruitless, as it happens), but it seems strange that the reportedly lengthy recording sessions in which Wings had been involved for most of the year had not resulted in a potential alternative.

In November, Ringo's *Goodnight Vienna* LP was released, along with a single taken from it, his revival of *Only You*, a song that had been a hit for both The Platters and The Hilltoppers during the 1950s. While it was somewhat less of a triumph than the *Ringo* LP, the album was still a big U.S. hit (although less so in Britain), while the single also reached the Top Ten, as did a follow up 45, *No No Song*, in America. In Britain, unfortunately, *Goodnight Vienna* and *Only You* became Ringo's chart swan songs, at least up to the time of writing.

George was also very involved in preparations for the release of his new LP and his first post-Beatle tour. These enterprises were so time-consuming that George decided against following Patti to Los Angeles, where she had gone to stay with her sister, Jenny, who was married to Mick Fleetwood of Fleetwood Mac, after her row with George over accepting a modelling job. George released the title track of his new LP, *Dark Horse* (which was also the inspiration for his choice of name for his record label) in America, and it reached the Top 20 as his U.S. tour (the first solo tour by any of The Beatles) began. Although the *Dark Horse* LP was evidently a success in America, reaching the Top Five and being certified gold, the tour received a fairly hostile reception, probably due in equal parts to the relentless religiosity of the majority of the songs George played and the presence of a number of Indian musicians sharing the stage with George and his excellent American backing band led by saxophonist Tom Scott and known as the L.A. Express. The fact that none of the Beatles had previously embarked on a solo tour of America resulted in a huge media spotlight focusing on George, which cannot have made the tour any less daunting, particularly when the critics were more or less unanimous in their condemnation. He was probably able to console himself (if consolation were necessary) with the thought that his records were still selling quite well in America, although the album was conspicuous by its absence from the British chart. To his credit, George had included on the LP, amid the dirges that made up most of it, a version of the classic Everly Brothers hit, *Bye Bye Love* with slight lyrical alterations that refer to 'our lady' (Patti) and 'old Clapper' (Eric Clapton), both of whom helped him to record the track. The packaging of the LP also mentions Olivia Arias, a Mexican-born secretary whom George first met at the time he was launching his own label in America, and whom he immediately hired to work for him. A few years later, she would become his second wife.

During the course of George's tour, John Lennon returned to the concert stage, although in most unlikely circumstances. Elton John, who had played on John's 'Walls And Bridges' a few months earlier, had told the latter that he was convinced that *Whatever Gets You Thru The Night* would become a Number One single. John initially scoffed, but when Elton remained adamant, Lennon agreed that if the record did top the chart, he would appear on stage with Elton's band. After the single had performed as Elton predicted, Lennon kept his part of the bargain by stepping on stage in New York unannounced at the end of November, and performed three songs, *Whatever Gets You Thru The Night, Lucy In The*

Above: John Lennon (right) in a relatively formal on stage appearance with Paul Simon.

Left: John Lennon's last live performance guesting with Elton John (left) at Madison Square Garden, New York on November 28, 1974.

Right: The 'official' version of the two sleeves in which John Lennon's 1975 album, Rock'n'Roll *was released.*

Sky With Diamonds and (somewhat ironically, since Paul had largely written the song), *I Saw Her Standing There.* The last of these recordings was released as the B side to Elton's *Philadelphia Freedom* single in early 1975, but the recordings of the other two songs were not released until early 1981, in the wake of John's murder. Of course, such matters would have been far from Lennon's mind at the start of 1975, by which time he had completed the recording of the album started in late 1973 with Phil Spector. By the autumn of 1974, John had regained the master tapes, but he was unhappy to discover that the vast majority of the tracks seemed somewhat ordinary. In fact, only four of the songs seemed fit to use, and towards the end of October 1974, John had spent an intensive week cutting new versions of ten of the tracks he had originally recorded with Spector. When the new sessions were completed, John felt that he had made an album of which he could be proud, and his record company agreed, although they suggested delaying the LP's release until April 1975, in order to get the maximum mileage from 'Walls And Bridges'. John agreed, but these plans were negated almost overnight, when an album was released by the mail order company, Adam VIII Records, titled *Roots – John Lennon Sings The Great Rock & Roll Hits.* This LP contained versions of virtually everything that was due to appear on the re-recorded LP plus two extra tracks John had decided not to remake, and was plainly made up of the recordings he had made with Spector.

At this point, the story becomes confusing. One of the tracks on the Adam VIII LP (and also one of the four Spector produced tracks which John had 'rescued' for the official version of his record) was *You Can't Catch Me*, a vintage Chuck Berry song. Berry's music publisher, a well known music industry entrepreneur named Morris Levy, had threatened to sue Lennon for plagiarism, as he felt that *Come Together*, from the *Abbey Road* album, was nothing more than a copy of *You Can't Catch Me* (a claim which seems to be not totally unfounded, by the way). To prevent himself being sued, Lennon had agreed to include several Chuck Berry songs on his oldies LP (whose original title, incidentally, was to have been *Oldies But Moldies* before it was altered to *Rock'n'Roll* some time prior to release), and in fact Berry's *Sweet Little Sixteen* was also included from the Spector sessions. Levy, no doubt spurred on by the continuing lawsuit over the similarity between George's *My Sweet Lord* and *He's So Fine*, was agitating for Lennon to keep his part of the bargain, to the point where John visited him at the end of 1974 to play him the recently reclaimed Spector recordings, and presumably left the tapes with Levy, having already decided to re-record most of them. Precisely why Levy then decided to release the Spector tapes in the form of a mail order album has never been made clear, but his claim that John and therefore Apple Records (to whom John was still theoretically signed) had verbally agreed to the release of the record, which was printed on the rear of the sleeve, was strenuously denied by John soon after the Adam VIII album came on the market. The official *Rock'n'Roll* LP's release was brought forward to February, as John and Apple sued Levy, who paid Lennon nearly $50,000 compensation during 1976, and obviously also took the Adam VIII LP off the market. Inevitably, sales of the official LP were affected, although it still made a quite substantial dent in the chart in both Britain and America, while the unauthorized LP, with the two tracks that were not on the official album, became a valuable collector's item. Little did anyone realize that it would be John's last new release until 1980.

The continuing saga of Wings, which had apparently become extremely unpleasant due to the inability of the two newest recruits, Geoff Britton and Jimmy McCulloch, to co-exist with even the semblance of peace, boiled over while the band were recording in New Orleans, and the unfortunate drummer was given his marching orders (although on what basis has never been made clear). A replacement was found quickly in the shape of an American named Joe English, who had become a well-known session musician after making an album with an obscure group known as Jam Factory. Shortly after English joined Wings, the group recorded a new single, *Listen To What The Man Said*, which was released during May as a 'trailer' for a new Wings LP, *Venus And Mars*. Eventually, both single and album topped their respective American charts, and the LP also reached Number One in Britain, although compared to the brilliance of *Band On The Run*, *Venus And Mars* was (and is) fairly ordinary.

Ringo had bought Tittenhurst Park, the Ascot mansion owned by John, but it soon became clear that even palatial new surroundings would be insufficient to save his marriage, and during July, he and Maureen were divorced on the grounds of Ringo's adultery with American actress Nancy Andrews, who thereafter lived with him for several years.

Ringo also continued with his film career, this time working as an actor in Ken Russell's overblown 'Lisztomania', which portrayed the classical composer Liszt (played by Roger Daltrey of The Who) as a teenage idol and also starred Rick Wakeman. Ringo's cameo role was that of the Pope.

John by this time had the confusion of the *Rock'n'Roll* albums behind him and the major story of the year was that Yoko had finally become pregnant – the Lennons had desperately wanted a child of their own ever since Yoko had miscarried during the late 1960s, and because she was no longer young and had suffered at least one miscarriage, it was felt by numerous doctors that it was unlikely that she could successfully bear John's child. However, by the summer of 1975, it was clear that she was pregnant, and as a result, John was granted a lessening of the pressure exerted by the U.S. immigration officials in that he was given temporary 'non-priority status'. For a change, the pressure

Left: The earlier unauthorized version of the Rock'n'Roll *album, with very different sleeve and slight variation of title.*

was off, at least temporarily, and John spent many hours ensuring that Yoko did nothing to jeopardize her pregnancy. During the early part of October an American Appeal Court quashed the order to deport John, and a few days later, Yoko successfully gave birth to a son, Sean Ono Lennon, who made his appearance on October 9. Having missed his son Julian's childhood largely due to the pressures of Beatlemania, John was determined that he would spend as much time as possible with Sean, and with a solid financial cushion available due to Yoko's shrewd investments, John was rarely seen in public for the next five years.

By the time of John's happy event, Patti Harrison had left her husband and eventually began living with Eric Clapton, although she and George were not finally divorced until 1977. It was unfortunate that the final breakdown of his marriage should have occurred just when George was at a low artistic ebb, with the less than triumphant *Dark Horse* LP on top of the relatively disastrous American tour. He may have been able to console himself with the fact that one of the groups signed to his Dark Horse label, a duo known as Splinter, had achieved a Top 20 hit with a catchy song, *Costafine Town*. Overall, though, the prospects for the label were little better than George's own, to judge from the mournful LP released during September, *Extra Texture (Read All About It)*, which was the final release to which he was contracted before being able to record for his own label. Whether this accounts for its very mundane qualities remains a quandary, although the LP was certified gold in America, and was certainly no improvement on George's run of insubstantial releases, despite the inclusion of a track titled *This Guitar* which is supposedly a 'continuation' of *While My Guitar Gently Weeps*, the excellent song George had written back in 1968 for the 'double white' album.

Paul was still enjoying the success of *Venus And Mars* until early September when he took to the road with Wings for a world tour that has been described as the most comprehensive ever undertaken up to that time – it lasted for thirteen months (with occasional breaks for recording and holidays), covered ten countries and was seen by over two million people. More to the point, although no one would have dreamed it at the time, the mammoth tour by Wings was the start of a five-year period during which the only erstwhile Beatle to do anything of great note was Paul McCartney, although in one or two

instances towards the end of the decade, the events in which he was involved reflected little credit on anyone. The final months of 1975 gave no real clue that John's solo career would enter a lengthy hiatus – his unpredictability during the earlier part of his life made it seem unlikely that he would stick to his resolution to retire during Sean's infancy – or that George, and especially Ringo, would be entering a commercially fallow period from which eight years later they would not have emerged. However, the end of 1975 did see the release of 'Best Of' albums from both John and Ringo, respectively titled *Shaved Fish* and *Blasts From Your Past*. John's album was the more successful in chart terms, despite being put together with less care than it perhaps deserved (for example, Phil Spector is credited as producer of *Cold Turkey*, which is incorrect), and even though *Blasts From Your Past* contained bigger hits (from an American point of view),

Below: Another demonstration of Ringo's versatility as an actor – after his earlier role as Frank Zappa in '200 Motels' here's the ex-Beatle playing the Pope in 'Lisztomania'.

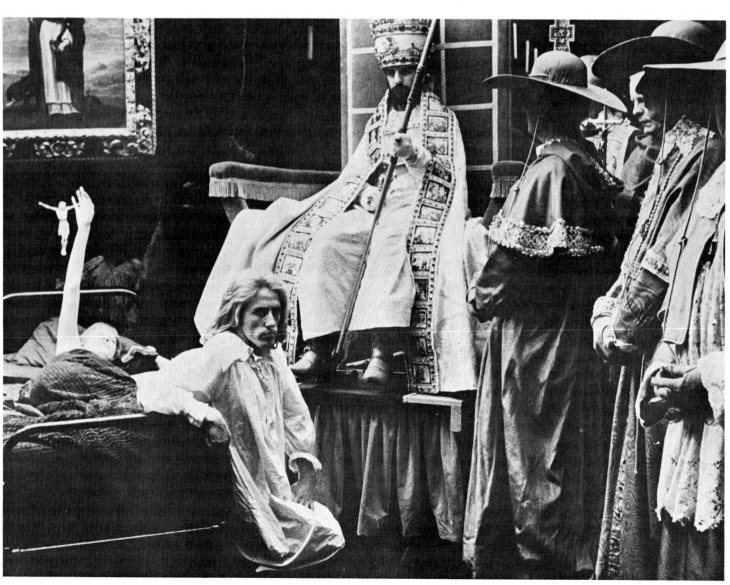

Above: Paul McCartney on stage with Wings in Cardiff during Wings' 1975/6 World Tour.

Shaved Fish peaked higher and remained in the chart for longer in the U.S.A., while Ringo's LP failed even to show in the British album chart. It was at this point that each of the solo recording contracts The Beatles had signed with EMI came to an end, and both George (who had his own label) and Ringo (who launched his, which he called Ring O'Records, although he seems never to have appeared on it himself, instead signing to the major companies who administrated his label) moved away from the womb-like confines of EMI in Britain and Capitol in America. John was unwilling to sign with anyone at this point, and only Paul was happy to continue with his existing arrangements, although before the end of the decade, he too would leave Capitol Records in America.

There were still hangovers from the EMI days at the start of 1976, like Ringo's single, *Oh My My*, and George's *This Guitar*, neither of which made any impact on the charts, although a major cloud came with the death of Mal Evans, the long-time friend and employee of each of the Beatles, who was by this time living in Los Angeles. Not long afterwards, and quite unexpectedly, an American concert promoter offered publicly the sum of thirty million dollars for a single concert by a re-formed Beatles, but the offer was ignored.

There was, however, a definite flavour of Beatlemania in the air, especially at the start of March. EMI released a set of records under the title of *The Singles Collection 1962–1970*, comprising the 22 previous Beatles singles in new picture sleeves, plus one new item, the first release in Britain of *Yesterday* as a single. Just how ready Britain was to welcome these reissues may be judged from the remark-

Paul and Linda on stage at Wembley in October 1976.

able statistic that all 23 singles approached (or in almost every case, re-approached) the chart, and *Yesterday*, the only 'new' 45, reached the Top Ten, although to put it in perspective, seventeen of the 23 only featured briefly in the unofficial U.K. Top 100. During the same month, Ringo signed with Atlantic Records in the United States and Polydor in Britain, and a new Wings LP, *Wings At The Speed Of Sound*, was released shortly before the American leg of the group's world tour, and spawned two very big hit singles later in the year. *Silly Love Songs* reached Number One in the United States and Number Two in Britain, while *Let 'Em In* was marginally less successful at Three in America and Two in Britain. The album was also a huge hit, topping the U.S. chart and all but equalling that achievement in Britain. It was an excellent calling card for what turned out to be a

highly successful debut tour of the U.S.A., which was also recorded and resulted at the end of the year in a triple live LP that topped the American album chart (a very significant feat for a three LP set) and made the U.K. Top Ten. America was also to some extent afflicted by the recurring spectre of The Beatles – a TV neo-documentary about mass-murderer Charles Manson was screened to a very interested public reaction, and Capitol Records decided to release a single coupling The Beatles song that Manson is said to have used as a blueprint for his murderous activities, *Helter Skelter*, with *Got To Get You Into My Life*. *Silly Love Songs* was at the top of the charts as The Beatles single was released, and its success may well have helped the reissue to reach the U.S. Top Ten as the first new single produced by the group in more than seven years.

Another shot from the Wembley concerts marking the end of the world tour by Wings.

EMI were so pleased with the sales of both the two double album compilations released in 1973 and the singles reissues that another double album was pulled together, under the title of *Rock'n'Roll Music*, and became a substantial hit without quite equalling the success of *1962–1966* or *1967–1970*, despite the extra impetus of *Back In The U.S.S.R.* being released as a single from the album, and reaching the British Top 20. Later in the year, this orgy of repackaging would continue with the release (for the first time in LP form in Britain, where it had previously been available as a twin EP set) of *Magical Mystery Tour*. However, by the time it was released, evidently comparatively few record buyers in Britain were very interested, perhaps because seven of the eleven tracks (certainly the most popular seven, at that) had already appeared on the *1967–1970* double album

three years before. With only Paul apparently active, the first in what would become a number of interview albums, featuring The Beatles talking, was released in Britain although an American LP titled *Hear The Beatles Tell All* had been released at the height of the initial American invasion back in 1964. The 1976 'spoken word' LP, *The Beatles Tapes – From the David Wigg Interviews*, contained no great revelations (the various interviews, all with individuals, were taped between 1968 and 1973) but briefly satisfied what was becoming a positive lust for new Beatles material on record. Curiously, the two group members who objected to the album and tried unsuccessfully to have it suppressed were George and Ringo. Paul, of course, was still involved in the mammoth Wings tour, while John finally received his 'Green Card', which allowed him to

The three concerts by Wings at Wembley climaxed what is claimed to have been the most comprehensive world tour ever, covering Britain, the rest of Europe, North America and Australasia during a fourteen-month period.

remain in the United States indefinitely, on July 27, and was quite reasonably far more concerned about that than a catchpenny LP of elderly interviews.

One business transaction involving Paul McCartney occurred during a break in the tour, when he acquired the music publishing company, E.H. Morris, for a substantial sum. Linda's family, who were looking after the business interests of the McCartneys, had urged Paul to invest part of his great wealth, although he had been unwilling to do so until he could feel some interest in the enterprise in which he was investing. An obvious outlet was to invest in some part of the music industry, and when Lee Eastman discovered that the vast majority of the songs written by Buddy Holly were administered by E.H. Morris, a company that might be persuaded to sell their copyrights, he informed Paul, whom he knew was a great admirer of the Texan rock'n'roller who had died prematurely in an air-crash. Paul was very excited by the news and wasted no time in authorizing the acquisition of the company, even going to some trouble and expense to present an annual 'Buddy Holly Week' each subsequent September, when films or concerts were usually presented to enthusiastic audiences.

Perhaps Ringo's objection to the David Wigg album had something to do with the

fact that he had decided (whether through a misunderstanding or not has never been established) to have his head shaved. At the time, Ringo was having an affair with Lynsey de Paul, a small but very attractive British songwriter/performer, alongside his longer-term relationship with Nancy Andrews, having just finished recording his next LP, *Ringo's Rotogravure*, which would be his first under the new contracts he had signed earlier in the year. Perhaps the excitement of all this activity confused him so much that he adopted the 'Kojak'

look without properly considering the consequences.

George, aside from his objections to the interview LP, adopted a very low profile for most of the year which eventually had unpleasant consequences, but not before the long-running law suit instituted by Bright Tunes had finally been settled in favour of the music publishers who administered *He's So Fine*. George was thus found guilty of plagiarism relevant to *My Sweet Lord*, and paid compensation to Bright Tunes of just under $600,000.

Ironically, Bright Tunes was by this time controlled by Allen Klein, and rather curiously, it was decided to reissue *My Sweet Lord* as a single in Britain for Christmas, 1976, although it failed to reach the chart.

Ringo's new LP, although no expense was spared in terms of star names – Eric Clapton, Peter Frampton, Dr. John and even John Lennon, who played piano on a song he wrote for Ringo, *Cookin' (In The Kitchen Of Love)* – and both Paul and George had also supplied material, was

During the mid-1970s, Ringo not only became a major celebrity in the capital cities of the world, but also went so far as to adopt a shaven-headed look. This informal game of backgammon with Peter Sellers took place in Monte Carlo.

notably less spectacular than its two pre-decessors. The absence of Richard Perry as producer was the most obvious difference, but to suggest that the change to Arif Mardin, a very experienced producer with a substantial list of hits to his name over a long period, was the major reason for the mundaneness of the album would probably be incorrect. It stiffed in Britain, as did the two singles taken from it, but in America, the LP reached the Top 30 and so did *A Dose Of Rock'n'Roll* when it was released as a single.

During September, as part of the world tour, Wings played before an audience of 40,000 in St. Mark's Square, Venice, donating the profits from the show to the fund set up to restore the famous city's buildings to their original splendour, and at the end of the year, the *Wings Over America* triple LP was released to huge popular acclaim, as already mentioned. 1976 had been a very successful year for

Paul overall, but unfortunately the same was not true of George Harrison, who not only lost the law suit over *My Sweet Lord*, but during the autumn found himself being sued by A&M Records, who ad-ministered his Dark Horse label. When he had placed Dark Horse with A&M, George had agreed that his first solo album on his own label would be ready for release as soon as he was free of his previous contractual commitments with EMI, but he had been suffering from hepatitis, and was unable to complete the album, $33\frac{1}{3}$, which A&M had scheduled for release on June 25, 1976, which was George's thirty-third and one third birthday. The company thereupon sued George for ten million dollars, seemingly taking the opportunity to cut their losses incurred in what must have seemed a disastrous investment in Dark Horse, almost all of whose releases were flops. Fortunately for George, his old pal Derek Taylor, with whom George had remained

Right: Denny Laine (left), Linda and Paul at a reception where they were presented with silver and gold discs for sales of their albums Venus and Mars, Wings At The Speed Of Sound *and* Wings Over America.

Above: The McCartney family pictured in Venice towards the end of 1976, when Wings played a benefit concert for the 'Venice In Peril' fund.

Left: Sleeve to the triple live album Wings Over America *which briefly topped the U.S. chart in 1977.*

close since the Apple days, was an executive at Warner Brothers Records, and jumped in on Warners' behalf to sign George, as a result of which A&M actually never released a Harrison solo record. The LP tickled the British charts and was a solid hit in America, where two singles from it, *Crackerbox Palace* and *This Song*, (apparently an explanation from George about his fear of writing songs after the *My Sweet Lord* judgement – it includes a line about not infringing anyone's copyright) both made the Top 30. For the moment, at least, George seemed to have rediscovered his direction to some extent.

Death, Drugs and Hope for the Future (1977-1984)

A rare picture of John and Yoko taken during John's self-imposed exile from music.

At the start of 1977, it seemed to Beatles lovers of all ages that there was at least a slim possibility of some kind of reunion of the group. After all, the schisms caused by Allen Klein were now behind John, Paul, George and Ringo, and on the evidence of solo records by each of them, plainly the whole was greater (at least in the eyes of record buyers) than the sum of its parts. John, of course, had decreed that he was not about to embark on any fresh musical endeavours until his son, Sean, was five years old (a vow that Lennon virtually kept, against all predictions), but it seemed possible, if not likely, that he might change his mind. George and Ringo obviously wouldn't object to a temporary reunion, at least as far as anyone could imagine, but would Paul be interested?

As it happened, Paul had other things on his mind, notably the fact that Linda was pregnant again, to which all intents and purposes meant that Wings would be unable to tour for most of the year. Although it has never apparently been confirmed, some portion of the early part of the year was spent by Paul on a somewhat curious project, an orchestral interpretation of his *Ram* album, which may possibly have been recorded some years, before, but for reasons unknown, failed to appear before 1977. The LP was credited to Percy 'Thrills' Thrillington, presumably an alias and popularly supposed by those claiming special knowledge to be Paul himself, although this priceless information was not circulated until some time later, by which time the LP was virtually unobtainable. Not long afterwards, another record involving Paul was also released, but only in America. *Seaside Woman* by Suzy and the Red Stripes was said to be actually a Linda McCartney single, on which she was backed by Wings, which was released by Epic Records, the label to which Paul would sign by 1979 – all notions of the identity of 'Suzy' had to be informed guesses.

The month of May 1977, saw a totally unexpected deluge of previously unreleased material by The Beatles as a group. First came the only 'official' live LP by the group, *The Beatles At The*

Hollywood Bowl, which consisted of tracks recorded at that venue in 1964 and 1965. At the time, they were regarded by George Martin and the group as technically disappointing, but the President of Capitol Records, Bhaskar Menon, unearthed the original tapes at the end of 1976, and invited George Martin to reconsider his decision of more than a decade before. Martin, while still unhappy with the technical aspects of the recordings, was reportedly most impressed with the energy displayed by the group, and agreed to work on the tapes with a view to their release commercially, although without any overdubbing of fresh vocal or instrumental parts. EMI Records in Britain, rightly recognizing the historical value of the finished LP, supported it with a £200,000 TV advertising campaign, as a result of which it briefly topped the British album chart, while in America it was certified gold on the day of release and platinum a week later. However, it must be stressed that although these actual recordings had never been previously released, little of note was contained in them, which was certainly

not true of the other album, a double titled *The Beatles Live! At The Star Club In Hamburg, Germany, 1962*, which contained recordings made on a small mono tape recorder with a hand-held microphone organized by Ted 'Kingsize' Taylor, a fellow Liverpudlian and contemporary of The Beatles during their Hamburg pre-fame days. Taylor was by this time working as a butcher in Liverpool, and he had offered the tapes, which were inevitably of poor quality, to Brian Epstein many years before for £20, but the latter had rejected the offer on the basis that the recordings were worthless, after which they were forgotten for many years until a recording engineer to whom Taylor had given them recalled leaving them in a derelict building, from where Taylor retrieved them. After offering them to both George and Ringo (the more accessible Beatles at this point) for £5000, but finding that neither Beatle was willing to pay what seemed a fairly inconsequential sum (probably because most of their assets were still tied up in the continuing saga of the winding up of Apple), Taylor finally sold the tapes to a record industry

Above: George Harrison became an enthusiastic motor racing buff during the late 1970s.

Opposite above: George with World Motor Cycling ace Barry Sheene (left) and veteran master of the circuits John Surtees discussing Sheene's imminent switch from two wheels to four, as he attempts to equal Surtees's feat of world success with both cars and motor cycles.

Opposite below: One of the many brilliant spoofs included in the TV show 'The Rutles'.

entrepreneur named Paul Murphy, and they were eventually licensed to the German-based Bellaphon label, who released them through a subsidiary known as Lingasong. Despite the reported £50,000 spent on 'cleaning up' the elderly tapes, the sound quality remains below par, but the fascination of hearing The Beatles as they performed prior to their huge fame makes the Star Club album a very interesting item, although this was not reflected at the time in sales, perhaps largely because The Beatles attempted to have the records withdrawn and suppressed by the courts. It was ruled in the High Court that the recordings were of historical interest, and the group's injunction was overruled, with the added comment from the presiding judge that action should have been taken before the album was put on sale, rather than after it appeared.

While all this Beatle activity was happening, George Harrison had finally found a new love in the shape of Olivia Arias, a Mexican-born secretary who worked for George's Dark Horse label. It is generally accepted that George and Olivia became more than friends when the latter recommended a Chinese acupuncturist to George at a point when he was becoming seriously ill and emaciated as a result of the problems he was experiencing with his marriage and his work, and after George's cure, he and Olivia became inseparable. She was undoubtedly a major catalyst in bringing George back into the reality of life after several years during which his devotions had devoured his time to the detriment of almost everything else, and although his relationship with the lady who later became his wife was of enormous benefit in many ways, it cannot really be said to have improved the sadly deteriorating quality of his new record releases. Nevertheless, George did develop some outside interests, notably a passionate involvement with Formula One motor racing. This is said to have been largely motivated by his admiration for Austrian driver Niki Lauda, who was involved in a fearsome crash in 1976 which came close to claiming his life, but who returned to the Grand Prix circuit only weeks later. George also involved himself with the team of comedians who became famous for TV shows and films under their collective name of 'Monty Python's Flying Circus'. George became particularly friendly with Eric Idle, and when Idle and some of his associates decided to make a spoof TV show on The Beatles about a group known as The Rutles (the name coming from a show starring Idle titled 'The Rutland Weekend Show'), George was pleased to appear in the show as an unnamed interviewer (while his own part – under the name of Stig O'Hara – was taken by erstwhile Beach Boy Rikki Fataar).

Ringo's year was fairly quiet – apart from cutting another fairly average album titled *Ringo the 4th*, which was little improvement on *Rotogravure* in assisting him to return to the success of his Richard Perry produced records, he apparently appeared in another film, 'Sextette', which also starred Mae West and Who drummer Keith Moon, but it seems doubtful whether the movie was released, or even completed. One outside project that did reach fruition, even though it was

probably of very limited interest to those who would normally be attracted to records by Ringo, was *Scouse The Mouse*, a concept LP based on a children's story written by British actor/film star Donald Pleasence. Ringo played the title role, while Adam Faith and Barbara Dickson took the other leading parts, and eight of the LP's fifteen tracks feature Ringo, although purely as a vocalist.

Most of the activity in the latter half of the year came from Paul – Wings worked on a new LP, originally to be titled *Water Wings*, but eventually released as *London Town*, as Linda's pregnancy progressed until she finally produced Paul's first son, James Louis, on September 12, just four days after Jimmy McCulloch left Wings, apparently because he felt that he wasn't being given any say in group decisions. Drummer Joe English also left Wings before the end of the year for similar reasons, and the group was back to its central core of Paul, Linda and Denny

Opposite: Paul and
Linda with their son
James Louis McCartney,
born on September 21,
1977.

Laine. In this stripped-down form, the trio had released an album earlier in the year titled *Holly Days*, composed of songs written by Buddy Holly, and released under Denny's name – obviously, drummers and lead guitarists weren't absolutely necessary for Wings, and with the virtually completed *London Town* album nearly ready for release, there was no urgency about finding replacements. During November, a new Wings single was released, titled *Mull Of Kintyre* and written by Paul about a place near his Scottish estate. While it was thought by many to be over-sentimental and utterly typical of the depths to which Paul could sink without the rougher touch of John Lennon, the single was an instant success in Britain (despite the inclusion of a band of bagpipe players whose appearance on the accompanying promotional video was hackneyed, to say the least) and topped the UK charts for nine weeks over the Christmas period, eventually selling more than a million and a half copies in Britain alone, and becoming the biggest selling single of all time in the United Kingdom. It also topped charts around the world, although

curiously it failed to penetrate the Top 30 in America. The end of the year also saw another double LP compilation of reissued Beatles tracks being released under the title of *Love Songs* (as a companion to the previous year's *Rock'n'Roll Music* double album), but the intensive repackaging of previous years, coupled with the only average response to the *Hollywood Bowl* LP, apparently prevented the huge sales that EMI in Britain and Capitol in America had been expecting.

If 1977 had seen a dearth of records from John Lennon, 1978 was the same, as John watched Sean growing and immersed himself absolutely in his domestic situation. George Harrison was also completely silent during the year, which he spent enjoying non-musical pursuits with Olivia, who, at the start of August, gave birth to a son which the couple named Dhani. A little over a month later, the happy couple decided to regularize their relationship by getting married, and George was said by everyone who met him to be as happy as they could ever remember. Probably the only cloud in an idyllic year came with the death of one of

Below: Paul (left)
conducts a trio of bagpipe
players during recording
of Mull Of Kintyre,
which became the biggest
selling single in Britain.
The picture was taken by
his wife Linda.

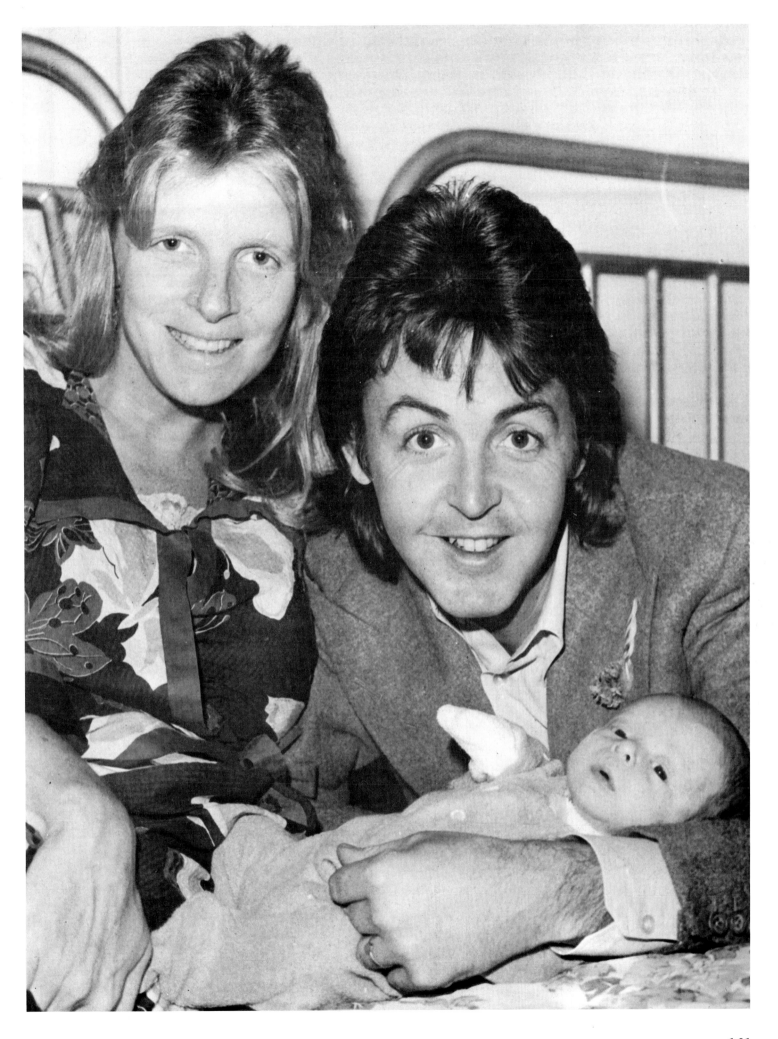

Right: Paul and Linda at the reception to launch the London Town *LP in 1978. Their long-time press representative Tony Brainsby looks on (right, with striped jacket).*

Below: Wings at the 1977 Capital Radio Music Awards Ceremony in London. Left to right, disc jockey Kenny Everett, Joe English, Paul and Linda, Jimmy McCulloch, Denny Laine.

Opposite: Proud parents George Harrison and Olivia Arias with their son Dhani, born August 1, 1978.

George's new friends from the motor racing world, Swedish driver Ronnie Peterson, in the year's Italian Grand Prix, but otherwise, George was very happy, having finally achieved some much needed stability in his tortured life.

Predictably, Paul was the busiest of the four ex-Beatles, releasing the *London Town* LP plus three singles taken from it – in every case, the releases were more successful in America than in Britain, and *With A Little Luck* topped the U.S. singles chart, while the LP reached Number Two in America and Number Four in Britain, although it is not remembered as one of Paul's best post-Beatles albums. At the end of the year, as Paul finally left Capitol Records in the U.S.A. and signed with Columbia (CBS), a compilation album with the title *Wings Greatest* was released on both sides of the Atlantic. Containing a selection of singles (for the most part), although some, like *Another Day*, were not recorded by Wings but by Paul as a solo artist, the LP performed better in chart terms in Britain than in America, although its relatively poor peak just inside the U.S. Top 30 may have resulted from yet another explosion of Beatles reissues.

During the summer, the burgeoning craze for picture discs (discs containing a built-in picture on the playing surface of the records) had resulted in the release of picture disc LPs of the *Sergeant Pepper* album, which was followed at the end of the year by similar releases of *Abbey Road* by The Beatles and *Band On The Run* by Paul and Wings. In addition the *1962–1966* and *1967–70* double albums were released in red and blue vinyl respectively, while *The Beatles*, the 'double white' album, was appropriately released pressed on white vinyl. Presumably aimed at Beatles collectors and completists who almost certainly already owned original copies of the various albums, these re-

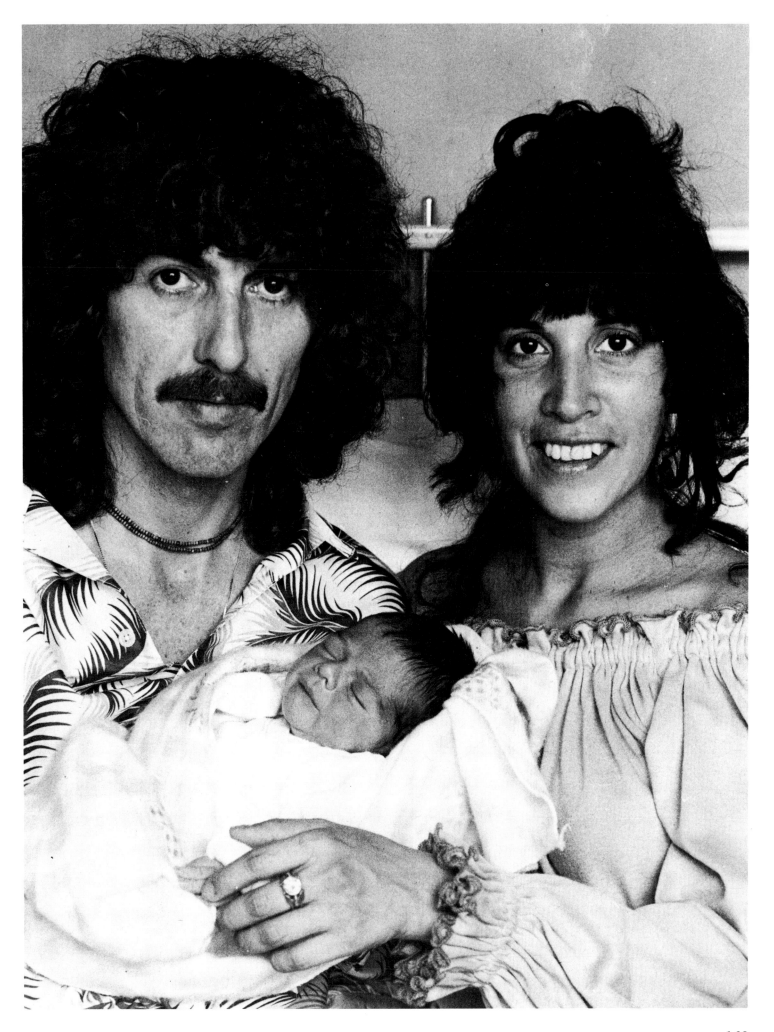

leases were little more than partially successful marketing ploys designed to maximize profits at little cost, and much the same could be said of a boxed set of Beatles LPs titled *The Beatles Collection*. The box contained twelve original albums plus a 'new' compilation titled *Rarities*, which, it was stressed, would not be sold separately. Since the set cost over £50 in Britain this made its acquisition something of a luxury, particularly when the *Rarities* LP was released at normal price, despite EMI's earlier decision, during 1979.

1978 was another year when Ringo Starr achieved very little. He released a new LP, *Bad Boy*, produced by Vini Poncia, an erstwhile associate of Richard Perry, but this change failed to halt his slide into commercial oblivion. However, many obviously felt that to have Ringo working on their records was still a mark of distinction – he was and is one of the finest drummers in the history of rock'n'roll, even if his vocals sometimes left something to be desired – and he played on a 'come-back' LP by Lonnie Donegan, the British 'King of Skiffle'

from the 1950s. In addition, his work as part of a star-studded band (including Bob Dylan, Neil Young, Joni Mitchell, Neil Diamond, Eric Clapton and Van Morrison) celebrating the final concert by The Band (known on record and film as 'The Last Waltz') was finally released.

The second half of the year also saw the recruitment of two new members for Wings, in the shape of drummer Steve Holly (ex of G.T. Moore and the Reggae Guitars) and guitarist Lawrence Juber, both of whom were recommended by Denny Laine. No one could have known that the group would soon be a thing of the past.

George Harrison was obviously delighted that he had finally become a father, perhaps not least because each of his erstwhile colleagues had at least two children, although to attribute his subsequent very limited output to the birth of Dhani would be to over-simplify the facts. After $33\frac{1}{3}$ in 1976, George released only three LPs of new material by the end of 1983, the first of them, at the start of 1979, using the imaginative title of simply *George*

A galaxy of stars – James Coburn (left), singer Lynsey de Paul, Ringo and Jack Nicholson. Lynsey was entangled romantically with both Ringo and Coburn during the later 1970s.

George (right) in 1977 with Elton John's percussionist Ray Cooper when George attended one of Elton's gigs in Paris.

Harrison. By all accounts, this album might have been even further delayed – George was not anxious to return to the recording fray and was sufficiently well-insulated financially by this time, even with Friar Park to support – had not his motor racing friends urged him to write a song about them. After his unfortunate experiences vis à vis *My Sweet Lord*, he was reluctant to embark on further composing projects, but eventually capitulated by writing *Blow Away*, which was released as a single during the spring of 1979, and as usual, performed far better in chart terms in America than in Britain. Similarly, the accompanying LP reached the Top 20 in the United States, but peaked briefly just inside the British Top 40, although it was actually marginally more lively than most of his recent output, including a song he had written for the 'double white' album by The Beatles ten years earlier, but which was never released in its original form, *Not Guilty*, plus *Faster*, another song with Grand Prix connections, as it was inspired by a book written by sometime world champion racing driver Jackie Stewart, whose title it shared. Later in the year, *Faster* was released as a single in Britain, both in

standard format and as an imaginative-looking picture disc featuring a collage of portraits of notable drivers – George donated all his royalties from the single to the Cancer Charity set up in memory of a driver who had died from the disease, Gunnar Neilson, but as it failed to chart, his gesture was somewhat fruitless. It would be nearly two years before a further new release.

As usual, Paul was the most active ex-Beatle in 1979, releasing a new LP recorded by the freshly assembled Wings plus several singles. *Goodnight Tonight*, the first single, seemed to augur well for the future when it reached the Top Five on both sides of the Atlantic. A concession by Paul to the then current 'disco music' movement, it was an excellent start for Paul's new American recording contract with Columbia, but was not included on the *Back To The Egg* album which appeared during the summer. The pattern of comparative failure in Britain and great American success was continued with the LP, which quickly achieved platinum status in the United States, but was only listed in the U.K. chart for less than four months, less than any of Paul's LPs since *Wild Life* at the start of the decade.

One interesting project that was previewed on the LP was the 'Rockestra', a concept Paul had conceived at the end of the previous year with a view to acquiring an orchestral sound of extraordinary density, perhaps ironically something like Phil Spector's 'Wall Of Sound' technique in which several musicians performed in unison rather than one player building up a dense sound by multiple re-recording and overdubbing. To achieve this, Paul invited such notable guitarists as Hank Marvin of the Shadows, Pete Townshend of The Who and Dave Gilmour of the Pink Floyd, extra drummers in the shape of Led Zeppelin's John Bonham and The Who's Kenny Jones, plus various bass and keyboard players and percussionists. The complete line-up amounting to two dozen people, although in truth the results were not as spectacular as Paul had perhaps expected. However, the 'Rockestra' concept would re-emerge at the end of the year, after a couple more singles from *Back To The Egg* had been issued to fainter interest than usual in America and rather less enthusiasm in Britain.

With no fresh news of John Lennon, other than the rumour that he might appear in a film titled 'Street Messiah' starring Olivia Newton-John, the big Beatles news of 1979 came during the summer, when Eric Clapton and Patti Boyd Harrison regularized their relationship by getting married finally. The actual ceremony took place in America, but towards the end of May, Eric and Patti decided to throw a huge party for their friends and families at their home near Guildford. Among the numerous celebrity guests were Jack Bruce and Ginger Baker, who, along with Eric, performed for the first time in more than a decade as Cream, while later on, Paul, George and Ringo found themselves on stage together for the first time in even longer. Although obviously a momentous occasion, it was strictly an ad hoc performance, of course.

Ringo had a very quiet year otherwise, largely due to a serious illness that afflicted him while he was living in Monte Carlo with actress Nancy Andrews, and resulted in surgeons removing several feet of intestine from his body. After his recovery, he returned to a life of 'international jet setting', as he himself referred to it, and during the summer, he played at the Claptons' wedding, and appeared in an all-star jam session on American TV along with Bill Wyman of the Rolling Stones, Todd Rundgren and Kiki Dee. He was even invited to open an Art Gallery in London, while George, who had similarly gone to ground after the early flurry of activity, was only mentioned in the newspapers for such nebulous items as a tractor running over his foot (obviously on a day crammed with vital news!) and his appearance in a motor race at Donington Park (he evidently didn't win).

*Left: The final Wings
line up (from left)
Lawrence Juber, Linda,
Paul, Steve Holly,
Denny Laine.*

*Below: Linda and Paul
dressed in Teddy Boy
gear at a party thrown
by Paul in honour of the
late, great Buddy Holly.*

1979 was definitely Paul's year as far as meaningful activity was concerned – September saw the annual celebrations for Buddy Holly Week, which were more spectacular than usual, culminating in a genuinely unforgettable concert at London's Hammersmith Odeon starring several members of The Crickets, Holly's one-time group, plus Don Everly and a galaxy of stars, including Paul and Wings, of course, performing together to a very enthusiastic reception. During the following month, he was honoured by Guinness Superlatives, the company who publish the various 'Guinness Book Of Records' series, who presented him with a 'rhodium disc' to recognize the 'fact' that he was the most successful songwriter and recording artist of all time, with 43 million selling records, more than 60 gold discs and more

Paul and Linda at the ceremony in London during October 1979, when Paul was presented with a rhodium disc as the most successful artist ever in terms of record sales.

record sales than anyone else in the world to his credit, although since The Beatles alone released over 200 different songs, almost all of which must have sold in excess of a million copies, the precise statistics on which the award was based seem at least a little peculiar. Shortly afterwards, Paul and Wings embarked on what would be their final tour of Britain, culminating in a free concert in Liverpool to which the pupils and staff of the Liverpool Institute, his old school, were invited. Everything was wonderful, or so it seemed, although a Christmas single, *Wonderful Christmastime*, which had originally been conceived back in 1969, was a complete flop in the United States, even though it deservedly reached the British Top Ten.

Ringo's year of misfortune continued when one of his several properties, his house in California, was gutted by fire, causing over £60,000 worth of damage, and incidentally destroying his collection of Beatles memorabilia. George's luck was better – the film he had helped to finance for the Monty Python team, 'Life of Brian', opened in London just before Christmas, becoming the top box-office attraction for several weeks, and eventually repaying George's investment (said to be two and a quarter million pounds) more than ten times over. No wonder he found it inconvenient to write and record on his own behalf.

Paul found himself involved in a much more serious undertaking – the country of Kampuchea had been afflicted by war, resulting in a vast number of deaths and many more starving, as a result of which, the Secretary of the United Nations, Kurt Waldheim, contacted Paul to ask whether the latter would appear in a charity concert whose proceeds might assist the plight of the Kampuchean people. Paul readily agreed, and helped to organize four nights of star-studded concerts in London, variously featuring Queen, The Who, The Clash, The Pretenders, Ian Dury and Elvis Costello, plus a final night appearance by Wings and a unique set from the reassembled 'Rockestra', this time twenty members strong and including three quarters of Led Zeppelin and half The Who as well as an augmented Wings. The one jarring feature of the entire event occurred when lawyers representing the various stars involved failed

to agree over various aspects of the marketing of the recordings and films made of the concerts, thus delaying the receipt of funds by those who needed them urgently in much the same way that George's 'Bangla Desh' contributions had been unnecessarily frozen.

The first year of the new decade would prove to be infinitely less congenial for Paul McCartney in the first instance, and by the end of the year, for the newly re-emerged John Lennon. It was a year when finally all suggestions of potential Beatles reunions would be forgotten, although this would not become clear until shortly before Christmas. At the start of the year, its tragic end could not be conceived, as Paul and Wings prepared to set off on a tour of the Far East in mid-January. Paul had not played in Japan since the final touring days of The Beatles, and the whole band were reportedly looking forward to absorbing some Eastern culture and enjoying the adulation of their many Japanese fans. Generally, Paul was not searched by customs officials when he entered a foreign country – why would a man reported to be one of the richest people in the world need to have his luggage scrutinized? On this occasion, the Japanese customs officer insisted that the entire McCartney clan – their children were with Paul and Linda – should open their suitcases, and in Paul's case, apparently without his knowledge, was a plastic bag containing nearly half a pound of marijuana. The police arrived and Paul was taken to prison, accused of attempting to smuggle the drug into Japan, a country where drug laws are particularly rigid. The British Consul informed him that his alleged offence was extremely serious under Japanese law, and that he faced a potential prison sentence of several years, but after ten days in jail, he was simply deported with the rest of the group, while the tour was obviously cancelled. As a result, Denny Laine supposedly informed Paul that he was leaving Wings, and not long afterwards, Steve Holly and Lawrence Juber also left.

It became clear that the incident in Japan was perhaps the culmination of a series of events that had alienated the departing trio – during the spring, a new single *Coming Up*, was released, which

Paul's remarkable Rockestra on stage on December 29, 1979, at Hammersmith Odeon. Recordings made during this series of concerts were later released on an album titled Concerts For the People of Kampuchea.

Above: Paul on his way to Japan for his ill-fated tour.

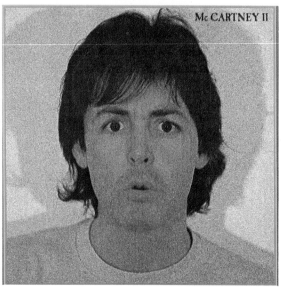

McCARTNEY II

Right: The sleeve of Paul's first post-Wings album, released in 1980.

topped the U.S. chart and reached Number Two in Britain. It had been recorded before the Japanese jaunt, but none of the other musicians had played on it, and the same was true of an almost totally solo LP, *McCartney II*, which was released soon afterwards. It was becoming gradually apparent that Paul had actually preferred to record by himself (with Linda adding backing vocals on one track of the LP) rather than instructing others what should be done. When the album topped the British charts a week after release, and a single taken from it, *Waterfalls* (in fact, the name of Paul's house in Sussex), reached the Top Ten, it could be seen that he was totally aware of what he was doing,

although curiously the LP was slightly less successful in the United States, and the single was a complete flop. A further single taken from the album was even a failure in Britain, but Paul, either by accident or design, or both, was again his own man completely.

After a largely inactive 1980, Ringo began filming 'Caveman', a movie about prehistoric times in which he starred with Barbara Bach (who had appeared in the James Bond film, 'The Spy Who Loved Me'). The two became romantically entangled, which resulted in Nancy Andrews, who had been Ringo's steadiest girl friend over the previous five years, commencing a law suit against her erstwhile lover for loss of her career prospects. Ringo and Barbara were unperturbed, especially when they survived a terrifying car accident in which Ringo's Mercedes (which he was driving at the time) turned completely over. Neither Ringo nor Barbara was hurt, barring a few scratches, and the accident served to cement their friendship into love.

Little or nothing was heard of George Harrison for almost the entire year, but the big news was that John Lennon was breaking his self-imposed five-year retirement, and had started recording a new album in New York. During his time away from music, John had undertaken the role of 'househusband', tending to his son Sean's every need, learning how to bake

home-made bread, and generally keeping to himself. He virtually exchanged roles with Yoko, who was in complete control of the couple's innumerable business interests, and apparently showed that she possessed considerable business acumen – not only did she evoke praise from Allen Klein for her handling of the continuing litigation involving the termination of the partnership among The Beatles and Apple, she also apparently invested so skilfully in real estate and agriculture that the Lennons by 1980 owned seven apartments in the ultra-exclusive Dakota Building in which they lived, and were also able to sell a cow from one of their prize dairy herds for a quarter of a million dollars!

Of course, by 1980, Sean was nearly five years old, an age at which he would start to attend school, when John could justifiably feel that he had properly overseen his son's earliest years, and could therefore return to making music without feeling any guilt. Yoko had not recorded either during John's lay off, and so they decided to make an album featuring seven songs by each of them, *Double Fantasy*, named after an orchid they had seen in a Botanical Garden in Bermuda during one of their family holidays. It would hardly be overstating the case to say that a new John Lennon record was the most eagerly awaited item in popular music, but when his first new single for half a decade, (*Just Like*) *Starting Over*, was released two weeks after his fortieth birthday (and Sean's fifth birthday), the public response was rather less than overwhelming. Inevitably, most people had expected some sort of masterpiece, but they had conveniently forgotten that since John's withdrawal from the firing line, there had been fairly dramatic changes in popular music spearheaded by the likes of Johnny Rotten, whose impact had been not dissimilar to that of The Beatles a decade and a half earlier. Perhaps everyone had assumed that John had kept in touch with changing musical fashions during the second half of the 1970s, but the awful truth (which only a few acknowledged) was that *Starting Over* was dangerously safe, and seemed to be the work of a sentimental and staid middle-aged man. After only four weeks on the British singles chart, the record began to drop, indicating that those who had purchased the single without hearing it far outnumbered those who bought it on merit. In America, where records take somewhat longer to peak, since chart positions are not totally related to sales, the 45 was still rising, although in smaller leaps than might have been expected in the circumstances. The chart performance of the LP, released a few weeks after the single, had been equally tentative, to the point that it had actually dropped out of the British Top 20, although it must be said that public reluctance was probably more due to the fact that half of the album was comprised of tracks featuring Yoko than to any particular shortcoming in John's new compositions, several of which seemed somewhat superior to the first single.

The return of John Lennon was proceeding, if perhaps more slowly than many had expected, and there was even talk of future live dates, although that would have to wait until he and Yoko had completed a further stint in the recording studio, largely taken up with a forthcoming single by Yoko, *Walking On Thin Ice*, which John was producing.

In fact, there had been very little in the way of public proclamations by John for almost the entire five years of his 'retirement', apart from an unexpected letter from him and Yoko, which appeared in the world's press in June 1979, and seemed to indicate that John was still tied up in neo-hippy idealism, but was somehow concerned that the world should be aware that he was still alive. The letter ended with the words: 'We are all part of the sky, more so than of the ground. PS. We noticed that three angels were looking over our shoulders when we wrote this!' Perhaps no one should have expected any dramatic changes in John's attitude, especially since he was back with Yoko, but what happened around 11.00 p.m. on the night of December 8, 1980, was completely unexpected – as John and Yoko returned to their apartment at the Dakota Building, there were two people, supposedly Lennon fans, waiting, whom John expected would ask, like so many others had in the previous weeks, for his autograph. One of the two, a young man who, it later transpired, had strongly identified with Lennon from his formative years, pulled out a gun and shot John five times. Lennon staggered into the door of

the apartment block, the doorman called the police, but John, who was bleeding profusely from his wounds, died on his way to the hospital.

His assassin was a 25-year-old named Mark David Chapman, born in Fort Worth, Texas, and raised in Georgia, who had been just one of many thousands of Americans captivated by The Beatles on their American debut in 1964, and had selected John for special adulation. His post school years had been spent firstly working as a missionary attached to the YMCA (he was said to be a 'born-again' Christian, at least at one time), after which he attended college, dropping out after a broken romance, and taking a post as a security guard in Hawaii, where he was trained in the use of firearms. While in Honolulu, he married a Japanese-American girl, but his Beatle/Lennon obsession continued unabated, and in October 1980, he left his wife and his job, and arrived in New York in early December, congregating with other Beatles freaks around the Dakota Building, hoping for a

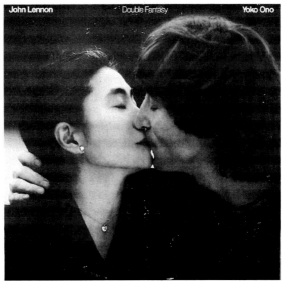

glimpse of John. He had reportedly acquired John's autograph on a copy of *Double Fantasy* on the afternoon of December 8, but only a few hours later, he pumped bullets in his idol, although to this day it has never been made clear why – Chapman's case seems not to have been reported since it was decreed that he should be incarcerated in a high security

Fans of John Lennon holding a vigil outside the entrance to the Dakota building where John was murdered.

prison for the dangerously insane, although it could easily be true that having murdered John Lennon, he may no longer be dangerous to anyone.

The news of John's death spread like wildfire – never since the death of Elvis Presley more than three years before had there been such media interest in a dead rock star. Yoko informed John's Aunt Mimi and Paul McCartney by telephone soon afterwards, but Cynthia, John's first wife, who was on holiday with Maureen Starkey, Ringo's first wife, didn't hear the news until several hours afterwards, whereupon Julian Lennon flew immediately to New York. George was told by his sister, who lived in America, and he instantly cancelled the recording sessions in which he was involved. However, Ringo was the only ex-Beatle who felt the necessity to go to New York, and he and

Barbara Bach spent time with Yoko and Sean as the world began to react to the death of a Beatle. Written tributes appeared at high speed and sold in prodigious quantities, and John's records began to move out of the shops faster than they ever had in his lifetime, with *Starting Over* briefly reaching Number One on both sides of the Atlantic, and *Double Fantasy* eventually doing the same, although not until the following February. Additionally, both *Happy Christmas (War Is Over)* and *Imagine* swiftly re-entered the U.K. singles chart, both selling more than ever before and peaking at Two and One respectively, the latter being replaced at the top after four weeks by another track taken from *Double Fantasy*, *Woman*, which eventually reached Number Two in America. There were dozens of tribute discs released, but per-

haps the only one of any substance musically was *Jealous Guy*, a song from *Imagine* tastefully performed by Bryan Ferry and Roxy Music, which deservedly topped the British singles chart in early 1981. A third single from the final album, *Watching The Wheels*, was released during April, but by that time almost every Lennon fan in the world must have owned *Double Fantasy*, so that the single's chart performance was relatively modest, although with terrible irony, Yoko's solo single upon which John had been working immediately before he was murdered, *Walking On Thin Ice*, became her first British chart hit, albeit a minor one.

Unsurprisingly, Paul, George and Ringo were devastated by John's death. George retrieved a song he had written for Ringo. *All Those Years Ago*, and rewrote the lyrics – Ringo had decided against

using the song in its original form, so George made it into a personal tribute to John, inviting Paul and Ringo to play on the track. When it was released during May, the single inevitably became George's biggest hit for eight years, and the LP from which it was taken, *Somewhere In England*, also served to briefly resurrect his chart career. Otherwise, George's year appears to have been almost totally involved with Hand Made Films, the company he had formed with members of the Monty Python team, which had another splendid year, helping to finance two major successes in 'The Long Good Friday' and 'Time Bandits'.

Ringo was little more active, although reviews of 'Caveman', the film in which he starred with Barbara Bach, were encouraging, and during April, he and Barbara were married at a London ceremony

Yoko accepting the Handel medallion on behalf of her late husband from the Mayor of New York, Ed Koch. The Handel medallion is New York City's highest cultural award.

175

Right: Sleeve of
Somewhere In England,
George Harrison's 1981
LP which included his
tribute to John Lennon,
All Those Years Ago,
which also featured Paul
and Ringo.

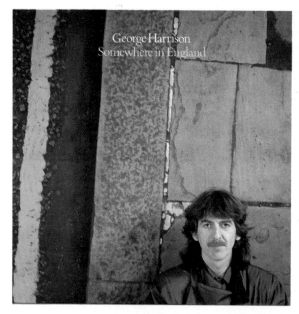

Right: Sleeve of Ringo's
late 1981 album Stop
And Smell The Roses.

Opposite: Ringo and
Barbara Bach with two
of their children from
previous marriages arrive
at their wedding
reception on 27 April,
1981. Paul and George
were among the wedding
guests.

draft and approved of it, apparently, although the completed film seems not to have surfaced subsequently.

Of the three surviving Beatles, Paul was inevitably the one with most reason to fear some kind of parallel to John's murder, and seemingly broke the habits of a lifetime by taking the sensible advice he was offered, which was to employ security guards at all times. For a while, he was content to do so, but eventually he became disturbed by constantly watching everyone around him in case they should turn out to be his Mark Chapman, and flew to the Caribbean Island of Montserrat, where George Martin presided over a high-quality recording studio, and overcame his paranoia during a lengthy period of assembling a new LP, although no new releases appeared during the year other than the *Kampuchea* album, about which the squabbles had finally ceased. For each of the survivors, 1981 was a year for low profiles.

1982 was little different for the most part – George and Ringo seemed to keep their heads down, while Paul achieved huge success, although not with his offer to purchase the Lennon & McCartney titles assigned to Northern Songs. Reportedly, the owners of the copyrights rejected his valuation of twenty-one million pounds, although on what grounds it is difficult to say. The other half of the celebrated songwriting partnership was obviously no longer affected by this type of aggravation – to prevent any argument over his will, he had simply inserted a clause that stated that if anyone tried to contest the amount he had left them, they would be omitted from the list of beneficiaries entirely – but Yoko found herself involved in a number of controversial law suits at this time. At the end of 1981, Jack Douglas, who had produced *Double Fantasy* and her *Walking On Thin Ice* single, successfully sued Yoko for non-payment of royalties.

His good humour can hardly have been improved by Yoko's decision to use Phil Spector as producer of her first solo album since John's death, *Season Of Glass*, whose sleeve was widely criticized for its apparent lack of taste, as it portrayed a pair of bloodstained spectacles believed to have belonged to John. Rumour has it that Yoko and Spector fell out sometime before the LP was finished,

attended by, among others, Paul and Linda, George and Olivia, Harry Nilsson and Derek Taylor. Later in the year, Ringo and his bride moved into Tittenhurst Park, the mansion in Ascot which he had purchased from John some years before, but two unfortunate events may have spoilt his year – early on, a design company he had formed closed down, but perhaps more damaging personally was the critical reaction to his first new LP for three years, *Stop And Smell The Roses*, which was described by one magazine as the worst record of 1981, a judgement which is a little harsh, but certainly gives some indication of the album's overall quality. Additionally, one of his ex-girl friends, Stephanie La Motta, wrote a movie script about her relationship with Ringo, which she titled 'Goodnight Vienna' – Ringo was invited to read the

Paul and Linda with comedian Billy Connolly at the launch party for Linda's book of photographs in September 1982.

but despite the fact that John was not represented either as writer or performer on the album (it was started after his death) save perhaps in spirit, it became Yoko's most successful LP thus far, at least in chart terms, briefly appearing in the Top 50 of the album chart in both America and Britain. It should be noted that at least half-a-dozen almost complete tracks had been recorded by John before his death, and Yoko effectively controlled their destiny – as a result, she was in a very strong bargaining position when dealing with record companies until 1984, when the unheard songs were finally released, in fact through Polydor Records.

Inevitably, John's death had increased sales of back catalogue Beatles records as well as Lennon's solo work, and 1982 saw the release of two 'new' Beatles LPs, the first an oddly conceived compilation with the title *Reel Music*, containing music from the group's five feature films. At the time, there was also a fashion for 'medley' records, where a number of an act's best-known songs were artificially linked together by producers and engineers, often by speeding up or slowing down original recordings to prevent jarring key changes and alterations in tempo. The acknowledged pioneers in this activity were a Dutch act known as Star Sound, in reality a group of session singers and musicians, who, under the guidance of Jaap Eggermont, one-time drummer with

a hit-making group called Golden Earring, assembled a medley with the title *Stars On 45*, using a substantial number of Beatles classics as the basis for the track. The single topped the U.S. chart, almost repeated the feat in Britain, and launched a short-lived but highly lucrative craze that a single taken from *Reel Music* and titled *Beatles Movie Medley* was intended to exploit, even though it was released some months after the medley craze had peaked. Nevertheless, the single came close to the Top Ten, even if the album itself was rather less successful. Later in the year, one of the very few configurations EMI had not used for repackaging Beatles material, the TV advertized *20 Golden Greats* concept, was also introduced, and even though there can have been very few people in the Western world who didn't already own virtually every track, it sold very well.

Perhaps more imaginative was the re-issue, in picture-disc form, of each of the group's original singles, released as close to the twentieth anniversary of their original issue as possible. *Love Me Do* finally became a Top Five hit in Britain using this method, although later releases in the series peaked much lower in Britain.

Despite the Beatle activity, 1982 demonstrated beyond all doubt that Paul McCartney was the one surviving Beatle with any commercial viability as far as hit records were concerned. In a flash of inspiration, he invited Stevie Wonder to collaborate with him on a single, *Ebony And Ivory*. Opinions of this track were polarized – some, this writer included, felt it trite and simplistically naïve in likening those with black and white skins to a piano keyboard 'together in perfect harmony', although it has been rumoured that there was less than perfect harmony during the recording session, due to Stevie Wonder's legendary ability to become side-tracked even when he had agreed to an appointment – he reputedly was so late for a dinner engagement with Paul and Linda that they had gone to bed by the time he finally arrived, although both he and the McCartneys were staying on the tiny island of Montserrat. No doubt this somewhat ungracious behaviour (if it actually occurred) was quickly forgotten when the record was released during the spring, as it was topping the British charts four weeks

later, and spent a remarkable seven weeks at Number One in the United States, selling in immense quantities. Its success was surely cemented by a clever promotional video that apparently featured the two principals performing the song together, although in fact they shot their parts on opposite sides of the Atlantic, the end result being one of the marvels of late twentieth-century technology. This celebrated duo also appeared together on another track, *What's That You're Doing*, which appeared together with *Ebony And Ivory* on Paul's *Tug Of War* LP during the summer. The album, which included participation from a number of distinguished musicians including 1950s rock star Carl Perkins, Eric Stewart of 10cc, jazz/rock bass player Stanley Clarke and Ringo Starr, was an equally predictable success, topping the LP charts around the world, although two subsequent singles taken

Below: Linda and Paul (right) with another famous married couple, Jean-Michel Jarre and Charlotte Rampling, at the Paris reception to launch a two-month exhibition of Linda's photos at the Canon Gallery in Paris.

from it were unsurprisingly smaller hits in view of the immense album sales.

Collaborating with Stevie Wonder had been such a success that Paul decided to further broaden his spheres by working with another black American whose popularity rivalled, or even perhaps exceeded that of Stevie Wonder. Michael Jackson had first come to prominence as the lead singer of his family group, the Jackson Five, even before he was a teenager, and in 1982 had been associated with chart-topping records for half his life. Nevertheless, to be invited to work with Paul McCartney was a distinction few shared, although it was agreed before Michael helped out with some of the vocals on the *Tug Of War* sessions that Paul would repay him in kind by appearing on Jackson's forthcoming *Thriller* LP. By the end of the year, a single appeared credited to Michael Jackson and Paul McCartney, *The Girl Is Mine*, written by Jackson but sung as a musical conversation (or perhaps competition would be more appropriate, as the protagonists were arguing over their proprietorial rights to a lady). It requires little imagination to realize that the single was a major hit.

For George and Ringo, the year was largely silent musically, although George's growing status as financier and executive producer of Hand Made Films was escalating – among the movies for which he was partially responsible were 'The Missionary', starring Michael Palin, 'Privates On Parade', featuring John Cleese among a stellar cast, and 'Scrubbers', directed by Mai Zetterling, all of which would become extremely successful at the box office as well as in critical terms. Ringo appeared in the feature film 'Yellowbeard', and was also connected

Below: Paul and Linda with Michael Jackson, who recorded duets with Paul that achieved major commercial success.

with an eleven-minute short titled 'The Cooler' with Paul McCartney, which was shown at the Cannes Film Festival and apparently released as a supporting item to 'Grease II'. The end of 1982 also saw a compilation album by John Lennon, *The John Lennon Collection*, released, following protracted negotiations between EMI, who owned the rights to the vast majority of his work, and Geffen Records, who had released the all-important *Double Fantasy*. EMI were doubtless ecstatic that the album topped the U.K. charts over the Christmas period, although Geffen Records, who released the LP in America, were somewhat less successful, at least initially.

1983 saw the pattern of the previous year virtually mirrored – a new album by George, *Gone Troppo*, was released shortly before the end of 1982 and widely ignored, and perhaps even more curiously, hardly publicized at all. His cinematic career, however, continued to prosper with the release of 'Bullshot', yet another comedy from the increasingly influential Hand Made Films. Most of the new releases were actually reissues of original Beatles singles in picture disc form, although their increasingly poor performance in chart terms must have suggested to EMI that many further twentieth anniversary reissues might lead eventually to negligible profits or even losses. Nevertheless, 1982 and 1983 had seen major recognition for The Beatles, after years of negotiation, in their home town of Liverpool. Four streets were named after individual Beatles, Mathew Street, in which The Cavern had stood, was the subject of redevelopment that would turn it into a 'Beatles shrine', and in 1983, 'Beatle City' was opened as a Beatles museum. By the end of the year, the surviving members of the group plus Yoko (representing John) were granted freedom of the city, and in New York, a portion of Central Park to be known as Strawberry Fields was officially opened by Yoko.

Ringo experienced mixed fortunes in 1983. He signed with a major American radio network to present a 26-programme series titled 'History Of The Beatles', although his new LP, *Old Wave*, produced by American rock guitarist Joe Walsh (late of The Eagles) was considered insufficiently commercial for release in

Left: Ringo pictured during a brief holiday in Tahiti, September 1982.

Below: Yoko and Sean Lennon on a pilgrimage to the famous children's home in Liverpool, Strawberry Fields, after which John named a famous Beatles song.

Above: Linda and Paul outside Uxbridge Magistrates Court when Linda was fined £75 for a minor drug offence.

Right: Sleeve to Milk and Honey, *the LP released in 1984 containing John Lennon's final original recordings.*

Britain, and was somewhat less than a huge success in the United States, although it was at least made available there. Musically, George was conspicuous by his absence, although the total lack of media activity concerning *Gone Troppo* made this unsurprising, and as usual, it was Paul who was most prominent. After spending a good deal of the first half of the year working on a film project, 'Give My Regards To Broad Street', for which he formed a group that included, apart from himself, Ringo, Linda and guitarists Dave Edmunds and Chris Spedding, he released a new LP, *Pipes Of Peace*, during the autumn, an early commercial highlight of which was another duet with Michael Jackson, *Say, Say, Say*, which was again a great success, while the title track of the LP released as a single topped the British charts in early 1984.

The end of 1983 brought news of several projects connected with John Lennon. His son Julian, by this time twenty years old, was signed by Charisma Records, who scheduled his recording debut for 1984, while a spoken word LP comprised of excerpts from John and Yoko's interview with 'Playboy' magazine was released, as a prelude to the final batch of unreleased tracks John had recorded before his murder. These appeared in early 1984 on an album titled *Milk And Honey* which was previewed by the release of a single, *Nobody Told Me*. Yoko and Sean also flew to London at the end of 1983 for a business meeting with George, Paul and Ringo, apparently to finalize arrangements for the winding up and total closure of the Apple empire, which had been the subject of complex and expensive litigation for over ten years.

Finally, it seemed, The Beatles were effectively no more, after nearly a quarter of a century during which they had conquered the world and been subjected to scrutiny more minute than any other act in popular music, and also more detailed than that accorded many whose work and achievements would appear to have been of infinitely more value. They deserved the adulation they received, if perhaps not the aggravation and lack of privacy – the continuing list of contenders and pretenders for the mythical title of 'The New Beatles' only serves to prove more conclusively with the passing years that their like will never be seen again.

Bibliography

There have been innumerable (some would say far too many) books published on and around the subject of The Beatles, individually and collectively. An exhaustive list would be of little use here, since many of the books are either inaccurate or dated. However, during the period when this book was written, the following reference volumes were consulted – the author believes them to be the most valuable books about The Beatles (not to mention the most accurate) and thanks those who wrote them for their invaluable ground work.

'Working Class Heroes', Neville Stannard (Virgin Books 1983). 'The Long and Winding Road', Neville Stannard (Virgin Books 1982). 'The Beatles: Who's Who', Bill Harry (Aurum Press 1982). 'John Lennon 1940–1980. A Biography', Ray Connolly (Fontana 1981). 'The Beatles Apart', Bob Woffinden (Proteus 1981). 'All You Needed Was Love', John Blake (Hamlyn Paperbacks 1981). 'A Day In The Life', Tom Schultheiss (Pierian Press 1980). 'Rock Family Trees', Pete Frame (Omnibus Press 1979). 'A Twist Of Lennon', Cynthia Lennon (W.H. Allen 1978). 'The Beatles: The Authorized Biography', by Hunter Davies (hardback – Heinemann 1968, 1978, McGraw-Hill: paperback – Mayflower Books 1969, Granada Books 1978). 'The Man Who Gave The Beatles Away', Allan Williams (Elmtree Books 1975). 'The Beatles: An Illustrated Record', Roy Carr & Tony Tyler (New English Library 1975).

Until such time as Paul McCartney writes his definitive autobiography (the same applies, although to a lesser extent, to George Harrison and Ringo Starr), the full and complete story of The Beatles may never be fully understood.

Filmography

The Beatles made (or were involved in) five feature films as a group, these being 'A Hard Days Night' (1964), 'Help!' (1965), 'Magical Mystery Tour' (1967), 'Yellow Submarine' (1968) and 'Let It Be' (1970). In addition, various compilations of Beatles performances are also in existence, among them the following: 'Around The Beatles' (a 1963 TV Special also starring Cilla Black and P.J. Proby), 'Washington Coliseum Concert' (1964), 'Shea Stadium Concert' (1965), 'Tokyo Concert' (1966) and 'What's Happening' (1967, a documentary about the group's first triumphant tour of the United States), as well as a commercially available video, 'The Compleat Beatles'.

Numerous films have used Beatles music as a soundtrack, including 'All This and World War II' (1976), 'I Wanna Hold Your Hand' and 'Sergeant Pepper's Lonely Hearts Club Band' (Both 1978) 'Birth Of The Beatles' (1979) and 'Beatlemania' (1981), although the group themselves do not appear on screen, and in most cases, their music is performed by others.

John Lennon's film career was dominated by his 'experimental' collaborations with Yoko Ono, although his solo debut came in 'How I Won The War' (1967). His movies with Yoko (most of which are reportedly repetitive and thus unwatchable), include 'Rape' (1969), 'Legs' (1970) 'Fly' and 'Apotheosis' (both 1971) and 'Erection' (1972, about the construction of a building, despite what the title might suggest!). Of rather greater interest are films in which he makes music – among these are 'Rolling Stones Rock'n'Roll Circus' (1968), 'Sweet Toronto' (1970, also known as 'Toronto Pop') and 'Imagine' (1972).

Paul McCartney's post-Beatle film career has been minor. Apart from numerous videos shot for promotional purposes (which will no doubt be assembled into a commercial video at some future date), 'Rock Show' (1979) is the only feature film in which he has appeared to date, although he has been involved in financing several cartoon features, such as 'Rupert The Bear', is part of the stellar cast of 'The Concerts For Kampuchea' (1981) and at the time of writing, had recently completed a new film in which he stars, 'Give My Regards To Broad Street'.

Aside from 'Concert For Bangla Desh' (1972), the film of the event which he organized, George Harrison has rarely been seen on film, other than in minor celebrity parts, although he has been connected either musically or in an administrative capacity with several movies. These include 'Wonderwall' (1968), 'Raga' (1971), 'Little Malcolm And His Struggle Against The Eunuchs' (1974) and 'The Rutles' (1978). More recently, his work as Executive Producer for Hand Made Films, the company formed with members of the 'Monty Python' team, has resulted in several major productions, including 'Life of Brian' (1979), 'Time Bandits' and 'The Long Good Friday' (1980), 'Monty Python Live At The Hollywood Bowl', 'The Missionary' and 'Scrubbers' (all 1982) and 'Privates On Parade' and 'Bullshot' (1983).

By far the most active Beatle in movie terms has been Ringo Starr, usually as a comic actor, but also as director, with 'Born To Boogie' (1972). He has occasionally taken starring parts, but the majority of his early credits were in supporting roles, many of them non-musical, although he also appears in George's 'Concert For Bangla Desh', Paul's 'Give My

Regards To Broad Street' and The Band's 'The Last Waltz' (1978). As an actor, the list of films in which he has appeared includes 'Candy' (1968), 'Magic Christian' (1970), '200 Motels' (1971), 'Blindman' (1972), 'That'll Be The Day' (1973), 'Son Of Dracula' (1974), 'Lisztomania' (1975), 'The Kids Are Alright' (1979) and 'Caveman' (1981).

Discography

Singles & EPs – UK *(official releases via EMI/Parlophone/Apple)* NR = NOT RELEASED

Year	Title	No.1	Top 10
1962	Love Me Do/P.S. I Love You		
1963	Please Please Me/Ask Me Why		★
	From Me To You/Thank You Girl	★	
	Twist And Shout (EP)		★
	She Loves You/I'll Get You	★	
	The Beatles' Hits (EP)		
	The Beatles (No.1) (EP)		
	I Want To Hold Your Hand/This Boy	★	
1964	All My Loving (EP)		
	Can't Buy Me Love/You Can't Do That	★	
	Long Tall Sally (EP)		
	A Hard Day's Night/Things We Said Today	★	
	Extracts from the film 'A Hard Day's Night' (EP)		
	Extracts from the album 'A Hard Day's Night' (EP)		
	I Feel Fine/She's A Woman	★	
1965	Ticket To Ride/Yes It is	★	
	Beatles For Sale (EP)		
	Beatles For Sale (No.2) (EP)		
	Help!/I'm Down	★	
	Day Tripper/We Can Work It Out	★	
	The Beatles' Million Sellers (EP)		
1966	Yesterday (EP)		
	Paperback Writer/Rain	★	
	Nowhere Man (EP)		
	Eleanor Rigby/Yellow Submarine	★	
1967	Penny Lane/Strawberry Fields Forever		★
	All You Need Is Love/Baby You're A Rich Man	★	
	Hello Goodbye/I Am The Walrus	★	
	Magical Mystery Tour (Double EP)		★
1968	Lady Madonna/The Inner Light	★	
	Hey Jude/Revolution	★	
1969	Get Back/Don't Let Me Down	★	
	The Ballad of John And Yoko/Old Brown Shoe	★	
	Something/Come Together		★
1970	Let It Be/You Know My Name (Look Up The Number)		★
1976	The Singles Collection 1962–1970		
	Yesterday/I Should Have Known Better		★
	Back In the U.S.S.R./Twist And Shout		
1977	The Beatles Collection (boxed set of singles)		
1978	Sergeant Pepper's Lonely Hearts Club Band/With A Little Help From My Friends/A Day In The Life		
1981	The Beatles EPs Collection (boxed set of EPs)		
1982	The Beatles Movie Medley/I'm Happy Just To Dance With You		★
	Love Me Do/P.S. I Love You (regular & picture disc)		★
	The Beatles Singles Collection (boxed set of singles)		
1983	Please Please Me/Ask Me Why (regular and picture disc)		
	From Me To You/Thank You Girl (regular and picture disc)		
	She Loves You/I'll Get You (regular and picture disc)		
	I Want To Hold Your Hand/This Boy (regular and picture disc)		

Releases *on labels other than EMI/Parlophone/Apple*

1962 *My Bonnie/The Saints* (with Tony Sheridan)
1963 *My Bonnie* (EP) (with Tony Sheridan)
1964 *Sweet Georgia Brown/Nobody's Child* (with Tony Sheridan)
1964 *Why (Can't You Love Me Again)/Cry For A Shadow* (with Tony Sheridan)
Ain't She Sweet/If You Love Me Baby
1977 *Twist And Shout/Falling In Love Again*
1982 *Searchin'/Money/Till There Was You*

Albums – UK *(official releases via EMI/Parlophone/Apple)*

1963 *Please Please Me*
With The Beatles
1964 *A Hard Day's Night*
Beatles For Sale
1965 *Help!*
Rubber Soul
1966 *Revolver*
A Collection Of Beatles' Oldies (But Goldies)

1967 *Sergeant Pepper's Lonely Hearts Club Band*
1968 *The Beatles* (double white album)
1969 *Yellow Submarine*
      Abbey Road
1970 *Let It Be*
1973 *The Beatles 1962–1966*
      The Beatles 1967–1970
1976 *Rock'n'Roll Music*
      Magical Mystery Tour
1977 *The Beatles At The Hollywood Bowl*
      Love Songs
1978 *The Beatles 1962–1966* (Red vinyl)
      The Beatles 1967–1970 (Blue vinyl)
      The Beatles Collection (boxed LP set)
1979 *Sergeant Pepper's Lonely Hearts Club Band* (picture disc)
      The Beatles (White vinyl)
      Abbey Road (Green vinyl)
      Let It Be (White vinyl)
      Magical Mystery Tour (Yellow vinyl)
      Hey Jude
      Rarities
1980 *The Beatles' Ballads*
      The Beatles Box (boxed LP set)
1982 *Reel Music*
      20 Greatest Hits

LP Releases *on labels other than EMI/Parlophone*
1964 *The Beatles' First* (with Tony Sheridan)
1971 *The Early Years* (with Tony Sheridan)
1976 *The Beatles Tapes From The David Wigg Interviews* (spoken word)
1977 *The Beatles Live! At The Star Club In Hamburg, Germany, 1962*
1981 *Hear The Beatles Tell All* (spoken word)
1982 *The Beatles Talk Downunder* (spoken word)
      The Beatles Interviews (spoken word)
      The Complete Silver Beatles

US singles and EPs *(released via Capitol or Apple unless otherwise stated)*

Year	Title	No. 1	Top 10
1963	*Please Please Me/Ask Me Why* (Vee Jay)		★
	From Me To You/Thank You Girl (Vee Jay)		
	She Loves You/I'll Get You (Swan)	★	
1964	*I Want To Hold Your Hand/I Saw Her Standing There*	★	
	Twist And Shout/There's A Place (Tollie)		★
	Can't Buy Me Love/You Can't Do That	★	
	Do You Want To Know A Secret/Thank You Girl (Vee Jay)		★
	Love Me Do/P.S. I Love You (Tollie)	★	
	Four By The Beatles (EP)		
	Sie Liebt Dich/I'll Get You (Swan)		
	A Hard Day's Night/I Should Have Known Better	★	
	I'll Cry Instead/I'm Happy Just To Dance With You		
	And I Love Her/If I Fell		
	Slow Down/Matchbox		
	I Feel Fine/She's A Woman	★	
1965	*4 By The Beatles* (EP)		
	Eight Days A Week/I Don't Want To Spoil The Party	★	
	Ticket To Ride/Yes It is	★	
	Help!/I'm Down	★	
	Yesterday/Act Naturally	★	
	We Can Work It Out/Day Tripper	★	
1966	*Nowhere Man/What Goes On*		★
	Paperback Writer/Rain	★	
	Yellow Submarine/Eleanor Rigby		★
1967	*Penny Lane/Strawberry Fields Forever*	★	
	All You Need Is Love/Baby You're A Rich Man	★	
	Hello Goodbye/I Am The Walrus	★	
1968	*Lady Madonna/The Inner Light*		★
	Hey Jude/Revolution	★	
1969	*Get Back/Don't Let Me Down*	★	
	The Ballad of John and Yoko/Old Brown Shoe		★
	Something/Come Together	★	
1970	*Let It be/You Know My Name (Look Up The Number)*	★	
	The Long And Winding Road/For You Blue	★	
1976	*Got To Get You Into My Life/Helter Skelter*		★
	Ob-La-Di Ob-La-Da/Julia		
1978	*Sergeant Pepper's Lonely Hearts Club Band/With A Little Help From My Friends/A Day In The Life*		
1982	*The Beatles Movie Medley*		

Albums – US *(released via Capitol/Apple Unless otherwise stated)*
1963 *Introducing The Beatles* (Vee Jay)
1964 *Meet The Beatles*
      Jolly What! The Beatles & Frank Ifield On Stage (Vee Jay)
      Souvenir Of Their Visit To America (The Beatles) (Vee Jay)
      The Beatles' Second Album
      A Hard Day's Night (United Artists)
      Something New

The Beatles vs. The Four Seasons
(Vee Jay)
*Songs, Pictures and Stories Of The
Fabulous Beatles* (Vee Jay)
The Beatles Story
Beatles '65
1965 *The Early Beatles*
Beatles VI
Help!
Rubber Soul
1966 *Yesterday And Today*
Revolver
1967 *Sergeant Pepper's Lonely Hearts Club
Band*
Magical Mystery Tour
1968 *The Beatles* (double white album)
1969 *Yellow Submarine*
Abbey Road
1970 *Hey Jude*
Let It Be
1973 *The Beatles 1962–1966*
The Beatles 1967–1970
1976 *Rock'n'Roll Music*
1977 *The Beatles At The Hollywood Bowl*
Love Songs
1978 *Sergeant Pepper's Lonely Hearts Club
Band* (picture disc)
The Beatles (White vinyl)
The Beatles 1962–1966 (Red vinyl)
The Beatles 1967–1970 (Blue vinyl)
Abbey Road (picture disc)
The Beatles Collection (boxed LP set)
1980 *The Beatles Rarities*
1982 *Reel Music*
20 Greatest Hits

US Singles *releases on other labels*

1962 *My Bonnie/The Saints* (with Tony
Sheridan)
1964 *Why/Cry For A Shadow* (with Tony
Sheridan)
*Sweet Georgia Brown/Take Out Some
Insurance On Me Baby* (with Tony
Sheridan)
Ain't She Sweet/Nobody's Child

US LP *releases on other labels*
1964 *The Beatles With Tony Sheridan and
Their Guests*
The American Tour With Ed Rudy
(spoken word)
Hear The Beatles Tell All (spoken
word)
Ain't She Sweet (with Tony
Sheridan and The Swallows)

1965 *Ed Rudy With New US Tour* (*The
Beatles Great American Tour*)
(spoken word)
*The Great American Tour – 1965
Live Beatlemania Concert* (spoken
word)
1966 *This Is Where It Started* (with Tony
Sheridan)
1977 *The Beatles Live! At The Star Club
In Hamburg, Germany, 1962*
1978 *Beatle Talk – The Way They Were
With Red Robinson* (spoken word)
1981 *Dawn Of The Silver Beatles*

John Lennon *solo and associated singles*

Year Title	UK No.1	UK Top 10	US No.1	US Top 10
1969 *Give Peace A Chance* (Plastic Ono Band)		★		
Cold Turkey (Plastic Ono Band)				
1970 *Instant Karma* (Plastic Ono Band)		★		★
1971 *Mother*	N/R			
1971 *Power To The People*		★		
God Save Us (Elastic Oz Band)				
Imagine	★			★
Happy Xmas (War Is Over)		★		
1972 *Woman Is The Nigger Of The World*	N/R			
1973 *Mind Games*				
1974 *Whatever Gets You Thru The Night*			★	
1974 *Number 9 Dream*				★
1975 *Stand By Me*				
1980 *(Just Like) Starting Over*	★		★	
1981 *Woman*	★			★
Watching The Wheels				★
1984 *Nobody Told Me*				

John Lennon *solo and associated LPs*
1968 *Unfinished Music
No.1 – Two Virgins*
(with Yoko Ono)
1969 *Unfinished Music
No.2 – Life With
The Lions* (with Yoko Ono)

The Wedding Album (with Yoko Ono)
Plastic Ono Band – Live Peace In Toronto 1969 (Plastic Ono Band)
1970 John Lennon/Plastic Ono Band
1971 Imagine
1972 Sometime In New York City (with Yoko Ono)
1973 Mind Games
1974 Walls and Bridges
1975 Rock'n'Roll
Shaved Fish (Collectable Lennon)
1980 Double Fantasy (with Yoko Ono)
1982 The John Lennon Collection
1983 Heart Play (with Yoko Ono) (spoken word)
1984 Milk and Honey (with Yoko Ono)

Paul McCartney *solo and associated singles*

Year Title	UK No.1	UK Top 10	US No.1	US Top 10
1971 Another Day		★		★
Uncle Albert/Admiral Halsey (with Linda McCartney)	N/R		★	
The Back Seat Of My Car (with Linda McCartney)			N/R	
1972 Give Ireland Back To The Irish (Wings)				
Mary Had A Little Lamb (Wings)		★		
Hi Hi Hi/C Moon (Wings)		★		★
1973 My Love (Wings)		★	★	
Live And Let Die (Wings)		★		★
Helen Wheels (Wings)				★
1974 Jet (Wings)		★		★
Band On The Run (Wings)		★	★	
Walking In The Park With Eloise (Country Hams)				
Junior's Farm (Wings)				★
1975 Listen To What The Man Said (Wings)		★	★	
Letting Go (Wings)				
Venus And Mars/Rock Show				
1976 Silly Love Songs (Wings)		★	★	
Let 'Em In (Wings)		★		★
1977 Maybe I'm Amazed (Wings)				★
Uncle Albert/Admiral Halsey (Percy Thrillington)			N/R	
Seaside Woman (Suzy And The Red Stripes)				
Mull Of Kintyre (Wings)	★			
1978 With A Little Luck (Wings)				
I've Had Enough (Wings)				
London Town (Wings)				
1979 Goodnight Tonight (Wings)		★		★
Old Siam Sir (Wings)			N/R	
Getting Closer (Wings)				
Arrow Through Me (Wings)	N/R			
Wonderful Christmastime		★		
1980 Coming Up (Wings)		★	★	
Waterfalls		★		
Temporary Secretary			N/R	
1982 Ebony And Ivory (with Stevie Wonder)	★		★	
Take It Away				★
Tug Of War				
The Girl Is Mine (wih Michael Jackson)		★		★
1983 Say Say Say (with Michael Jackson)		★	★	
Pipes of Peace	★			

Paul McCartney solo and associated LPs
1970 McCartney

1971 *Ram* (with Linda McCartney)
Wild Life (Wings)
1973 *Red Rose Speedway* (Wings)
Band On The Run (Wings)
1975 *Venus And Mars* (Wings)
1976 *Wings At The Speed Of Sound* (Wings)
Wings Over America (Wings)
1977 *Thrillington* (Percy Thrillington)
1978 *London Town* (Wings)
Wings Greatest (Wings)
Band On The Run (picture disc) (Wings)
1979 *Back To The Egg* (Wings)
1980 *McCartney II*
The McCartney Interview (spoken word)
1982 *Tug Of War*
1983 *Pipes of Peace*

George Harrison *solo and associated singles*

Year	Title	UK No.1	UK Top 10	US No.1	US Top 10
1970	*My Sweet Lord*	★		★	★
1971	*What Is Life*	N/R			
	Bangla Desh		★		
1972	*Give Me Love (Give Me Peace On Earth)*		★	★	
1974	*Dark Horse*				
	Ding Dong				
1975	*You*				
	This Guitar (Can't Keep From Crying)				
1976	*This Song*				
1977	*Crackerbox Palace*	N/R			
	True Love			N/R	
1979	*Blow Away*				
	Love Comes To Everyone				
	Faster			N/R	
1981	*All Those Years Ago*				★
	Teardrops			N/R	
1982	*Wake Up My Love*				

George Harrison *solo and associated LPs*
1968 *Wonderwall Music*
1969 *Electronic Sound*
1970 *All Things Must Pass*
1971 *The Concert For Bangla Desh* (with others)
1973 *Living In The Material World*
1974 *Dark Horse*
1975 *Extra Texture (Read All About It)*
1976 *Thirty Three & ⅓*
The Best Of George Harrison
1979 *George Harrison*
1981 *Somewhere In England*
1982 *Gone Troppo*

Ringo Starr *solo and associated singles*

Year	Title	UK No.1	UK Top 10	US No.1	US Top 10
1970	*Beaucoups Of Blues*	N/R			
1971	*It Don't Come Easy*		★		★
1972	*Back Off Boogaloo*		★		★
1973	*Photograph*		★	★	
	You're Sixteen		★	★	
1974	*Oh My My*				★
	Only You				★
1975	*No No Song*	N/R			★
	Snookeroo			N/R	
	It's All Da Da Down To Goodnight Vienna	N/R			
1976	*A Dose of Rock'n'Roll*				
1977	*Wings*	N/R			
	Drowning In The Sea Of Love				
1978	*Lipstick Traces*				
	Heart On My Sleeve	N/R			
	Tonight			N/R	
1981	*Wrack My Brain*				
1982	*Private Property*	N/R			

Ringo Starr *solo and associated LPs*
1970 *Sentimental Journey*
Beaucoups Of Blues
1979 *Ringo*
1974 *Goodnight Vienna*
1975 *Blasts From Your Past*
1976 *Ringo's Rotogravure*
1977 *Ringo The Fourth*
1978 *Bad Boy*
1981 *Stop And Smell The Roses*
1983 *Old Wave*

Index

Figures in italics refer to
illustration captions